MW00648166

Your First Year in CTE:

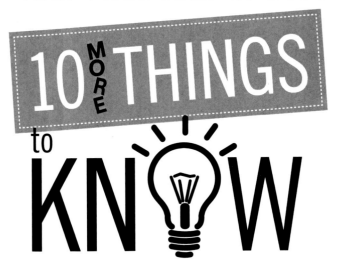

ISBN# 978-0-692-56791-3

Published by the Association for Career
and Technical Education

Association for Career
and Technical Education

ACTE

1410 King Street Alexandria, VA 22314
Phone: 800-826-9972 // Fax: 703-683-7424
www.acteonline.org // *Connecting Education and Careers*

Table of
Contents

Important Note: We realize that some of you may be getting some additional professional development help from any one of many potential sources. You may be starting that metamorphosis from technician or clinician to professional career and technical education (CTE) educator. Though we have maintained our "lighthearted" approach to this book and its chapters, we wanted you to understand that the chapter layout is grounded in solid pedagogical sequencing.

- Chapters I and II address curriculum and planning.
- Chapters III and IV address classroom instructional strategies and CTSOs.
- Chapters V and VI address assessment and instructional improvement.
- Chapters VII through IX address how to deal with external populations common to CTE.
- Chapter X addresses the practices of reflective planning and good management.

about the
Authors

Much like those of *Your First Year in CTE, 10 Things to Know,* the authors of this book have more than 150 years of CTE experience and represent a broad range of perspectives and roles within that field. In addition, the contributing authors have 150 years of knowledge and experience totaling more than 300 years of career expertise.

Dr. John Foster's career experience began when he was a tradesman in the construction industry. In the early years of the Vocational Education Acts, a community college career counselor had John visit a carpentry program in a regional school. Soon after that visit he began his career in CTE as a carpentry teacher. At the time, John was a bit of a rarity: he had a bachelor's degree in vocational education as a starting teacher. He later earned a master's degree in vocational education administration and became a CTE director at the secondary level. John completed a Ph.D. in workforce development and began work in CTE teacher education. It was in these two positions that he witnessed the positive power of instructional improvement through the objective use of data. Dr. Foster took a position as a state director of CTE and served under three different governors. Dr. Foster also formed relationships with a number of key researchers in the field of CTE; among them were Dr. Ken Gray, Dr. Neil (Mac) McCaslin and Dr. James Stone. John credits the many stars of CTE that he has met along the way for sharing their expertise, and hopes his experiences will benefit those reading this book. In 2005, Dr. Foster took the helm of NOCTI, formerly the National Occupational Competency Testing Institute, and while there has forged strong ties with the National Association of State Directors of Career and Technical Education consortium (NASDCTEc) and the Association for Career and Technical Education (ACTE).

Dr. Pamela Foster obtained her bachelor's and master's degrees in science education and later a Ph.D. in workforce education and development. She taught in a comprehensive (academic and CTE) high school for 34 years, during which she was also the science program chair for 12 years. As a science representative, Pam worked with and mentored academic and CTE educators to create motivating and integrated lessons and units. She has shared her experiences and practices at local, state and national conferences. Pam has facilitated webinars for the Southern Regional Education Board (SREB) and was responsible for planning integrated nationwide professional development activities. She was recognized in 1991 as a semi-finalist for state teacher of the year and was recognized as outstanding biology teacher in 2010 by the state of Pennsylvania. Although retired, she continues to mentor new CTE teachers and volunteers with the Audubon Society in teaching grade-school students about STEM-related issues, including stream ecology and conservation.

Dr. Clyde Hornberger is a dynamic leader whose wide-ranging list of experiences included the institution of competency-based instruction in the largest technical program in the state of Pennsylvania. He served as executive director of Lehigh Career and Technical Institute for more than 15 years, during which he doubled the institution's offerings and established the school as a national model. Clyde also served as president of the Pennsylvania Association of Career and Technical Administrators (PACTA) and served on the executive boards of the Pennsylvania School Board Association (PSBA), the Manufacturing Skill Standards Council (MSSC) and the SkillsUSA leadership council. He earned his doctorate in education at Temple University and previously held teaching and administrative assignments in CTE in Schuylkill and Berks Counties. Retired Colonel Hornberger also maintains the discipline and focus on outcomes that he learned throughout his military career. Clyde served as special advisor to the Pennsylvania Secretary of Education for almost 10 years. He was appointed to the Pennsylvania House of Representatives Keystone Commission on Education for Employment for the 21st Century. He has also served as chair of the NOCTI board of directors. Clyde's focus throughout his career has been to enhance the educational and career opportunities for youth, incumbent workers and adults. He currently serves as an educational consultant specializing in CTE, and has been a consultant for the school districts of Philadelphia, Little Rock, St. Louis, Anchorage, Omaha and a number of others.

Dr. Kathleen McNally is a school improvement specialist for SREB, specifically working with high schools and technical centers to operationalize the *Technology Centers That Work (TCTW)* Ten Key Practices and Key Conditions. She has worked as a high school mathematics teacher, as associate director of training for national SkillsUSA, in higher education in a university workforce education and development program as a CTE teacher educator and as the director of CTE for the Milton Hershey School. Kathleen has worked with new and seasoned CTE teachers while partnering with them as a colleague on student projects and assignments and by supporting them in their quest for teacher certification. She helped teachers navigate the challenges and rewards of being a CTSO advisor. Dr. McNally's work with SREB involves working with states on embedding mathematics in CTE instruction, including facilitating the adoption of the Mathematics Design Collaborative (MDC) tools and frameworks. She also works with faculties to implement Project Based Learning (PBL) instructional/planning approaches, and facilitates TCTW and *High Schools That Work* (HSTW) efforts across the network.

setting the
Stage

We recently rediscovered an article originally written for the California New Teacher Project and published back in 1990 by the California Department of Education. The topic of the article was challenges for new teachers and those challenges were categorized into four phases. The article described them generally as survival, disillusionment, rejuvenation and reflection; it explained that all four of these form a process that occurs over a single year. The popular wisdom regarding those who come to education through alternative certification routes is that this process probably repeats itself during several of the early years and that the disillusionment phase may extend throughout multiple years. Even for the most experienced of our alternatively certified CTE teachers, this disillusionment phase can have an impact on instructional effectiveness. So, why did we choose to "Set the Stage" with what appears to be a prediction of doom and gloom for new teachers? The answer lies in making sure that all of us engaged in the process of preparing new CTE teachers, and the new teachers themselves are aware of these cycles. Not only should you be aware of these cycles—you should also expect them! If you can move past Phases 1 and 2, Phases 3 and 4 will make you a better and happier CTE professional. We believe you'll see that *positive attitude* reflected in some of our chapters and you'll be able to see that others have gone through the same experiences that you are having.

Our partner book entitled *Your First Year in CTE: 10 Things to Know* focused on those first three months of an individual's new teaching career. It is no coincidence that the aforementioned California article calls this first phase of new teaching: "Survival." It is a time when new teachers are instantly and frequently bombarded with problems and situations they had not anticipated. Even with the benefit of a four-year degree in teaching pedagogy, new teachers generally find themselves consumed by day-to-day activities and find it difficult to make time to plan. These new teachers are still uncertain as to what strategies will work with their students. It is important to note that typically these new teachers have not only had the benefit of a degree in education methodology, but they may have also had a student teaching experience. Compare and contrast the difficulties of that population by examining the experiences of an alternatively certified CTE teacher.

We talked in our first book about CTE teachers being a special breed. The factors that account for that "specialness" may also account for some of the frustration experienced in that first year. Because this second book is still about one's first year in CTE, we have chosen to reiterate how this "specialness" can be a mixed blessing by repeating a small section about the characteristics of CTE teachers from the first book.

- CTE teachers typically begin their teaching careers at an older age than most teachers of regular education. This may mean that they have gotten accustomed to what has been, up until a point, a routine that has made them effective and efficient in their respective CTE occupations. In the classroom, they may suddenly find that they are no longer effective. Do you see why they might get frustrated?
- CTE teachers typically bring many years of content experience with them before they enter the classroom. That content experience, however, is not in education and suddenly they can't rely on the background that has made them successful in their former careers.
- CTE teachers make substantial career changes in order to enter the classroom. Oftentimes, they are at the top of their particular field and they transition into a career they know little about, starting over at the bottom rung.
- CTE teachers make a commitment to a lifetime of education. Not only do they have to maintain currency in the technical field that each one has left, they must also play "catch up" in the new field. In many states, alternatively credentialed CTE teachers have to acquire a substantial number of college credits in teaching pedagogy while simultaneously working in a new field.

These four differences alone create a ripple of effects that make it more difficult for CTE teachers to navigate their new environment.

The first book was targeted at developing relationships and surviving the first three months. We mentioned that without proper support, some of these difficulties may cause those entering a new field to give up and return to his or her former field. Even those who have support and a good initial "launch" may end up working so hard to succeed that "burn-out" becomes a real issue. The research literature and folklore surrounding CTE teaching indicate that this attrition occurs in the first three to four years for teachers new to CTE teaching. We hoped that a lighthearted approach might help them.

This book is meant to maintain an "easy and fun" approach for newer CTE teachers; but like its predecessor, it should be a great resource for the veteran CTE teacher too. The "hands-on" examples can provide teachers in regular education classrooms with ideas that can be adapted for their classrooms as well. We want this to be one of those books you'll enjoy reading, but we also hope that you will keep the information, examples and resources nearby for use in your teaching.

We also want to continue to gather great examples of "Tools for Your Toolbox" on ACTE's support website at www.acteonline.org/FirstYearInCTE. In this way, the entire CTE community can benefit from your examples.

We know that CTE teachers are a special breed! If you are new to our field, we want to welcome you to what we hope becomes your new passion. It certainly did for us!

chapter I
What We Teach

The road less taken: Teaching as a career path

When you ask teachers why they do what they do, whether they have been on the job for several years, several months or even several days, some common themes emerge. One compelling reason that individuals take on the responsibilities of teaching is a desire to "give back" to society by working with future generations; to contribute to his or her technical field by developing human capital for a highly skilled American workforce. Teaching was probably a respected profession in your experience, and you probably had influential teachers whom you looked up to and appreciated. Perhaps a certain teacher affected your life deeply and positively, and just maybe you developed a desire to be that positive influence for others.

The authors know that CTE teachers have the opportunity to pass on occupational skill, knowledge and experience to the next generation. They can make a contribution to the economic vitality of the local labor force and, most importantly, make a difference in someone's life.

Consider these paraphrased thoughts regarding the impact of a teacher's actions:

- To teach is to touch a life forever. (Author unknown)
- Education is not preparation for life; education is life itself. (Attributed to John Dewey)
- Children are living messages we send into a lifetime we will not see. (John W. Whitehead)
- It is the supreme art of the teacher to awaken the joy in creative expression and knowledge. (Albert Einstein)
- Education is not the filling of a pail, but the lighting of a fire. (William Butler Yeats)

So often, it is not financial reward, benefits or recognition that fuels a career choice to teach tomorrow's leaders. It is truly meaningful and rewarding to help students harness their full potential and give back to society by investing in future generations. This commitment to the profession is an important influence, especially for this chapter's topic, "What we teach." CTE is responsible for many outcomes—improving students' technical competence, employability skills, economic independence and inspiring a love of learning. CTE teachers have great responsibilities, too. When they are committed to their responsibilities as educators and to excellence, then what they teach can bring deep value and unique benefit to students' lives, as well as a positive effect on the world around them.

CTE in the past: A quick review of our evolution

The Association for Career Technical Education (ACTE) understands all too well the role that CTE has played in preparing students and workers for the workplace, and how that role has changed to address the evolving needs of business and industry. Schools specializing in preparing workers for certain jobs began to surface in the 1800s. In 1879, the first manual training school opened, combining hands-on training with classroom learning. As the country's agricultural economy grew, so too

Historical Snapshot

did the need for agricultural education, which fueled greater acceptance of "vocational" schools. Federal funding and focus on *vocational education* increased consistently for almost 50 years, but World War II created a need for technical skills on a scale that hadn't been seen before. Our nation had an urgent need for skilled workers for defense and the need continued after the war to retrain citizens to re-enter the workforce.

In the 1960s, federal legislation not only embraced these concepts, it extended them. In those years, the government provided funding to allow states to focus monies on facilities to enhance *vocational education*. Some states focused on funding to technical colleges, some on programs based in existing high schools, but many focused on the building of regional centers focused primarily on secondary students. These regional centers represented a new way of thinking about educational governance and the funding of complex technical programs.

Vocational education, as it was called at the time, was intended to help prepare students for work. *Vocational Education in the United States: 1969-1990* (Hoachlander, Kaufman, Levesque & Houser, 1992) describes an important evolution regarding the intent of this educational methodology, as follows, "Although vocational education is intended to help prepare students for work, both inside and outside the home, many educators and policymakers believe it has a broader mission: to provide a concrete, understandable context for learning and applying academic skills and concepts. To this end, the Carl D. Perkins Vocational and Applied Technology Education Act of 1990 called on schools to integrate vocational and academic education" (p xviii), and this theme of integrated instruction is still maintained in the federal Perkins Act today.

Context and history are always important factors when making decisions and when framing personal philosophies, so in addition to an understanding of the federal legislation that drove CTE, it is important to understand different types of CTE teachers and how they were prepared for their careers. This book was written as a resource for those entering CTE without the benefit of a teaching degree, a direction most states refer to as an "alternative" route to becoming a teacher. Teachers who have entered the profession via the alternative route may think that route to be the only one that exists. However, there are others and, as a new CTE teacher, it will help you to have a general sense of how your fellow teachers might have been prepared for their jobs.

During the 1960s and 70s there were seven categories of vocational education teachers (Hochlander et al., 1992) and each represented a slightly different method of preparation (Zirkle, Martin & McCaslin, 2007). These seven areas also link directly to career and technical student organizations (CTSOs), which are discussed in greater detail in Chapter IV:

- Agricultural education teachers were traditionally prepared with a combination of agricultural courses and teaching courses by a college or university granting a four-year degree. They typically also participated in a student teaching experience prior to full-time employment as a teacher.

- Business education teachers were traditionally prepared with a combination of business courses and teaching courses by a college or university granting a four-year degree. They also typically participated in a student teaching experience prior to full-time employment as a teacher.
- Distributive education teachers, like their business education counterparts, were prepared by four-year institutions. Their focus, however, was on marketing and the "distribution" of goods.
- Health education teachers were unique in that, though many had completed a four-year degree program, the program emphasis was on aspects of anatomy, physiology and patient care with little focus on pedagogy.
- Family and consumer science teachers were traditionally prepared with a combination of family and consumer (formerly home economics) courses and teaching courses by a college or university granting a four-year degree. Typically, they participated in a student teaching experience prior to full-time employment as a teacher.
- Technical education teachers were traditionally prepared with a combination of technical (formerly industrial arts) courses and teaching courses by a college or university granting a four-year degree. Typically, they participated in a student teaching experience prior to full-time employment as a teacher.
- Trade and industry teachers are the group that typically utilized the "alternative" certification route. Most did not have a degree encompassing educational methodologies, but typically had many years of occupational experience covering all aspects of a particular industry. In some states, these individuals acquired a permanent teaching credential as they simultaneously entered CTE and earned a teaching credential.

Generally speaking, the difference in preparation between these seven subgroups lies in the fact that five of them enter CTE through a traditional teacher preparation route and two of them typically enter without that experience (Zirkle et al., 2007). Instead, these alternatively certified individuals bring with them many years of content experience.

This difference in preparation also impacts the availability of industry-specific textbooks. For example, although there are a number of textbooks for business education teachers, a wind turbine technician teacher has fewer options. This usually translates for those alternative-route teachers into having to prepare something called a "job and task analysis" (JTA). This JTA was an analysis of everything that needed to be conveyed to students so they could enter their chosen field (Brown, 1997). This JTA became the

culum outline for many alternatively credentialed teachers. An
set of steps for completing a JTA appears in the toolbox section
_.., chapter.

CTE—The present: The current landscape also shapes what we teach

At the time of this writing, CTE is in the national spotlight as a key strategy to address the mismatch between high-wage, high-skill work opportunities and what students learn in their educational programs to prepare them to be highly skilled workers. CTE as an educational strategy continues to gain attention as an effective means of workforce development:

> Increasingly, many CTE methods and strategies of learning in the context of the real world are being applied in traditional education courses. The key difference is with consistency around the word "both." CTE programs are designed to help students meet both academic (mathematics, English Language Arts, science, etc.) and career-field technical content standards with real-work experience. The technical content standards are revised, generally every five years, by panels of educators and business/industry representatives and are embedded with the academic content standards. (Ohio Department of Education, 2015)

American Educator (Fall 2014) includes articles from a number of scholars and practitioners adding their voices to this important conversation. As the lead author (Stone, 2014) notes:

> In recent years, a well-intentioned push for all students to earn four-year degrees has resulted in limiting, rather than expanding, educational opportunities. A strictly academic curriculum has been prioritized to the detriment of career and technical education (CTE), which provides the link between the needs of the labor market and the needs of young people to be prepared for life after education. Because of its potential to engage students, CTE is now experiencing renewed interest as a viable option for students both career and college bound.(p. 2)

In fact the seven classifications for CTE teacher preparation and CTSOs have evolved to a system that is focused largely on economic sectors, called clusters (National Association of State Directors of Career Technical Education Consortium, 2015). While some states have adopted variations of the Cluster model, nationally there are 16 clusters and they are:

- Agriculture, Food & Natural Resources
- Architecture & Construction
- Arts, A/V Technology & Communications
- Business Management & Administration
- Education & Training
- Finance
- Government & Public Administration
- Health Science
- Hospitality & Tourism
- Human Services
- Information Technology
- Law, Public Safety, Corrections & Security
- Manufacturing
- Marketing
- Science, Technology, Engineering and Mathematics
- Transportation, Distribution & Logistics

These economic clusters were introduced in the late 1990s and can be broken down further into approximately 90 "pathways" and still further into jobs. In the Architecture and Construction Cluster, for example, one would find three pathways: Design/Preconstruction, Construction and Maintenance/Operations. Within the construction pathway, you find the job of carpenter, for example. Depending upon your school and the state in which you are located, programs could be defined by pathway, job, theme or academy, each definition helping you to understand the basics of the origin of the program you are teaching and its expectations regarding specificity of content.

Additionally, when you think about the question, "What am I to teach?" and you consider historical and current influences, it is also helpful to consider the context of your own set of life experiences. How have you gained the knowledge, skills and understanding that have made you a technical professional?

If you are a graphic designer, perhaps your current skill set includes knowledge and skills like the list below:

- An ability to sketch out ideas and concepts
- Use of Adobe Illustrator
- An understanding of color theory
- An ability to conceptualize thoughts and ideas from others
- Communication with clients
- Knowledge of typography
- Creation of a multi-colored, three-dimensional template
- Communication of specific details of a job to a subcontractor
- Use of balance in visual layout

Notice that there is an interesting "mix" of what someone needs to know, what they need to be able to do and what learning is necessary for success on the job. You may see indications of different types of knowledge and skills on your list, such as technical (use of Adobe tools), academic (color theory) and foundational skills (communication). These skills actually fall into three separate categories or domains, which are described later in Chapter V. In essence these domains are about thinking, doing and feeling. If you consider what students need in order to be successful in your industry today, you can bet it will be all of those. The content of a CTE program or course is a combination of what students:

- Need to know—concepts, theories, habits of mind
- Need to understand—explain how something works, apply a theory to a problem
- Be able to do—hands-on skills and techniques to complete tasks, create, repair, etc.

The spotlight is bright: Benefits of CTE

CTE has evolved from a sole focus on procedural skills with an "I model, you watch, then you do" instruction to one that empowers students to take more ownership in their learning, make decisions, learn independently, work in teams and solve authentic problems. Quality CTE programs provide an amazing opportunity for students to learn authentically and innovate and solve "real-world" problems. Add to that the opportunity to gain independence and confidence, which also comes from working both in teams and individually to solve both small and large problems. CTE has a proven record of success with students at all levels, not only secondary students, but also as a cost-effective educational opportunity for postsecondary students and adults who seek specific training and skills.

Ultimately, all education leads to work, whether that work involves medical skills in a hospital, welding skills in a manufacturing plant or designing skills in an office. Most CTE teachers would agree that their responsibility is not only to prepare students to enter a career, but also to provide their students with skills to advance in that career and to have a successful future. With that in mind, dissect what a student will need to learn to be able to handle the following:

A customer calls for service to his hot water heater, which has suddenly stopped working. The heater is an older model and a makeshift connection feeds to an outdoor wood boiler. As the HVAC technician on call for the business, you will need to figure out how to troubleshoot the heater, repair it on site and prepare a report capturing the work done and the costs involved.

Taking a moment to analyze the skills and knowledge the HVAC technician needs in this scenario, the answer would certainly include technical understanding of different hot water heater models and the hands-on skills to repair the problem. Our analysis would also include academics, such as communication skills and mathematics (for measurement and proportion). CTE programs are an effective way to help students acquire a full range of knowledge. Think of it as learning skills and acquiring a knowledge base to produce a product, engage in a process and provide a service!

What we ask students to do is directly related to their motivation to succeed. Course content, together with instructional and assessment strategies, can support students as they gain essential knowledge, skills and understandings. So, it's worth paying attention and not leaving the decision of "what to teach" to chance.

CTE teachers and programs can play a vital role in realizing this for students and for our country's workforce as they provide value-added learning opportunities using authentic, work-based problems and contextual projects that support innovation and provide meaning to students. We know that a combination of technical and academic skills in tandem with personal development opportunities provide deeper learning. Keeping this in mind will help inform decision making about what to include in your program's goals and related content. As a new CTE teacher, you will need to articulate why what you teach is important and to advocate for the benefits of CTE to your existing and potential students. What you are teaching is much more than how to turn a wrench. What you teach must be reflective of career preparation, not just the process of job preparation!

Now that you have some basics under your belt, the next chapters will begin to discuss the planning process, both long term and day-to-day. These chapters are not meant to be a step-by-step recipe, but rather a menu of considerations that, regardless of your CTE program type, you can utilize to construct and maintain quality instruction for your students.

Tools for your toolbox

In this chapter we discussed what it is that CTE teachers teach, how they develop content and what influences what they do in the classroom. The toolbox section is included in all of the chapters and it contains both reflections from CTE teachers and templates or guides that you might be able to use in your career. The first "tool" in this section is a reflection about the importance of your life's experiences and the rewards one gets from engaging in teaching others a skill.

My career in education and as an instructor of CTE began in a strange way. When I graduated from high school, I was undecided about what to do in my life. It was during the 'hippy generation', the Vietnam era and an active military draft lottery. Going to college as a full-time student with a class load minimum of twelve units earned an individual a draft deferment. The decision most male high school graduates had to make at the time was go to school or go to war. My initial selection was to choose school.

I entered community college near my hometown not knowing what I wanted to study, but knowing two things: I didn't want to be a cop, because my dad was a career policeman, and I didn't want to be a teacher. Other than those two careers, my mind was open. While in high school I had taken a number of industrial arts courses each year and had especially enjoyed my drafting classes. I decided to major in architecture. I am still not sure why I made that decision, I was actually more suited to be an engineering major, but what does a high school senior know about either of those two careers? Architecture it was.

During my second year in community college, I had dropped a class, fell below the required twelve units, had a low draft lottery number (meaning I had a high probability of being drafted), and I had received my draft notice. So to make sure I had some choice in my upcoming military service, I ran down and joined the Air Force. With my education in drafting, the Air Force decided to train me to become a carpenter. Three and a half years later, after one tour overseas, getting married and discharged from the military, I returned to school to complete my education.

My wife began work full time, I found a part-time job and I was able to use the GI Bill to help support the cost of finishing my education. But there was a problem. The architecture program at my chosen university was now very difficult to get into. I was faced with another major decision: switch universities or change careers. The military experience had helped me mature, my marriage had focused my mind on long-term sustainable employment in order to support my future family and so I decided, if I can't finish my career in architecture, I will use my experiences to help others pursuing careers in architecture and construction. Thus began my 40-year career as a CTE teacher, administrator and state director of CTE.

What was the biggest reward for me? Knowing that I helped to train many individuals to be successful architects. In fact, I was able to help many individuals find successful and meaningful careers, something of which I'll always be proud!

This reflection focuses on the rewards of having been in a profession that gives people the ability to be successful, but it also talks about the value of one's experiences. Earlier in the chapter, we mentioned the importance of understanding how to begin to analyze your occupation to find the critical components your students need for success. Many texts have been written about JTA, and it is not our intention to go into any particular method in any detail.

However, the listing of some basic steps may help bring some clarity to which tasks are critical to your students' success:

STEP 1: Collect Information about the Job
Review any materials that describe the occupation; consider sources like the *Dictionary of Occupational Titles* and any previous job descriptions to which you might have access.

STEP 2: List the Tasks
Prepare a list of what you did on the job that made you successful; these major components within a job are usually referred to as "tasks."

STEP 3: Identify the Critical Tasks
Take some time to review this list of tasks. Make sure that you have captured them all and then begin to think about the importance of each one. This rating could be based on the number of times it was performed or by how critical the task was.

STEP 4: Identify the Critical Competencies
A competency is usually considered a subset of a task. Analyze each task and break down the competencies involved in completing the task. Once they are identified, you'll notice some commonalities, such as accuracy of measurement or use of a common tool. You'll find that those competencies appearing frequently are usually deemed essential. Devise a scale to rate all the competencies; even labels as simple as "nice to know" or "critical to know" will help.

STEP 5: Connect the Tasks and Competencies
As a last step, connect the competencies and tasks. By doing this you may also find tasks that are not connected to critical competencies or have no

competencies connected to them at all. These are tasks that should be eliminated from any instruction, as should those "nice-to-know" competencies.

If you are a new CTE instructor and your state or school has not provided direction on your program of study (POS), and/or your curriculum is not aligned to any textbook resource materials, this simple guide will help in analyzing your own experiences and determining the critical skills that will make your students successful.

We've also asked a long-serving assistant state director from Missouri about his reflections on the field of CTE. We think that it serves to underscore the importance of the profession you have chosen to become involved in and the emphasis on what constitutes a successful career.

Over the past 28 years, I have had the opportunity to work with and observe CTE teachers in a number of different capacities. There is no more noble profession than that of teaching and especially teaching in the area of CTE. The role of a CTE teacher has changed dramatically over the years. In the past, CTE teachers were primarily responsible for teaching technical skills and focused on those students who were headed directly to the workforce after high school.

Now, with the changing labor market needs and the realization that more jobs require further and more complex training beyond high school, CTE teachers must have a solid understanding of academics and their application in the real world as it relates to student's chosen career paths. They teach those same technical skills but with more attention being paid to underlying academic theories and workplace readiness skills, or as many refer to them—'soft skills'.

Many CTE teachers come into the profession directly from business and industry. They bring a totally different perspective to the classroom that many of their academic counterparts do not. They understand the important connections and also the value that CTE brings to the overall educational experience for students.

KEY LEARNINGS:

1. CTE teaching is about giving back.
2. Our CTE history influences what it is that we teach.
3. Federal legislation combined with federal dollars influence what we teach.
4. The economy (national, state and local) influences what we teach.
5. There are numerous ways to enter the CTE teaching profession and each of those ways influences what we teach.
6. Job and Task Analysis can help in prioritizing what we teach.
7. The relationship between clusters, pathways and jobs is important.
8. CTE is about solving real-world problems and applying both skills and knowledge to do so.
9. CTE is about preparing for life and careers more than it is about any single job.

REFERENCES:

Association for Career and Technical Education (ACTE). (2015). History of CTE. Available at www.acteonline.org/general.aspx?id=810#. Vdx4z5fvfh4.

Brown, B. L. (1997). Task Analysis Strategies and Practices. Practice Application Brief. ERIC Number: ED404571. Available at http://eric.ed.gov/?id=ED404571.

Hoachlander, E. G, Kaufman, Levesque, P. K. & Houser, J. (1992). *Vocational Education in the United States: 1969-1990.* NCES 92-669. Washington, DC: U.S. Department of Education, Office of Educational Research and Improvement. Available at http://nces.ed.gov/pubs92/92669.pdf.

National Association of State Directors of Career Technical Education Consortium. (2015). Available at www.careertech.org/career-clusters.

Ohio Department of Education. (2015). Career Tech FAQs. Available at http://education.ohio.gov/Topics/Career-Tech/CTE-FAQ#FAQ1517.

Stone, J. R. III. (2014, fall). More Than One Way: The Case for High-Quality CTE. *American Educator, (38)* 3. Available at www.aft.org/sites/default/files/ae_fall2014.pdf.

U.S. Department of Labor and Social Policy Research Associates. (2011, March). *Career Pathways Initiative: Building Cross-Agency Partnerships* (webinar recording). Available at www.workforce3one.org/view/3001107557559061701.

U.S. Department of Labor and Social Policy Research Associates. (2011, September). *Career Pathways Toolkit.* Retrieved from https://learnwork.workforce3one.org/view/2001134052969836533/info.

Zirkle, C. J., Martin, L., & McCaslin, N. L. (2007, October). *Study of State Certification/Licensure Requirements for Secondary Career and Technical Education Teachers.* St. Paul, MN: National Research Center for Career and Technical Education, University of Minnesota. Retrieved from www.nrccte.org.

Note:

The Carl D. Perkins Career and Technical Education Act of 2006 (Perkins) calls upon states to create sequences of academic and CTE coursework to help students attain a postsecondary degree or industry-recognized certificate or credential, otherwise known as a program of study (POS). At minimum, according to the definition put forward in Perkins, programs of study must:

- Incorporate and align secondary and postsecondary education elements.
- Include academic and CTE content in a coordinated, non-duplicative progression of courses.
- Offer the opportunity, where appropriate, for secondary students to acquire postsecondary credits.
- Lead to an industry-recognized credential or certificate at the postsecondary level or an associate or baccalaureate degree.

chapter II
Annual Planning in CTE

Planning is bringing the future
into the present so that you can
do something about it now.
–Alan Lakein

Have you ever known someone who
seems to "ride by the seat of his or
her pants" and seems to "shoot from
the hip" when faced with a decision
or a task? It is tempting to take a sort
of spontaneous approach to life when
we are faced with so many unknowns
and variables. Even though setting a
course may sometimes feel a bit fu-
tile, we need to be able to plan—but
plan with flexibility.

Flexibility is a key skill for any
teacher, because days are rarely
the same and often not what you'd
planned. But by a teacher's failing
to invest in "big picture" planning
for your instruction, students may
meander through assignments and
activities that don't add up to deeper
learning. Planning *what* you will
teach, and *when* and *how* students
will demonstrate their learning may
be a bit foreign compared to the expectations in your previous work expe-

Where is
MapQuest when
you need it?

riences. But, if you are willing to consider "planner" as an important role in the life of a teacher, this chapter will offer some tips, tools and techniques to help you map out successful experiences for your students. So, let's see what planning a learning journey is like!

Consider your customer: How students learn

When thinking through how to plan your courses and daily activities, it helps to consider both how students learn best and your philosophy of how to teach well. The following principles may help you with decisions on what to include in your plans:

- Plan instruction to build on students' strengths—consider their expertise and learning styles (see resources section for fun inventories). Plan so that students can demonstrate their expertise to their peers through student-led teaching opportunities; the outcome will be more invested, engaged learners.
- Consider a variety of instructional strategies (see Chapter III) that allow for collaborating, reflecting, solving problems and applying academic knowledge. Open-ended projects are a super way to incorporate hands-on experiences with high-level thinking tasks.
- Invite students through problem solving and project-based learning (PBL) approaches (see resources section for websites) not to work through a "lock-step" series of tasks, but to consider, plan, design, test, implement, revise and communicate their accomplishments, bringing depth to assignments.
- Consider how your community can act as an extended classroom. Can students visit job sites and see firsthand how their skills are utilized on the job? Will there be opportunities for students to showcase their skills and knowledge by participating in internships or providing service to the community?
- Think about how you will evaluate your students' progress. (Student assessment information is contained in Chapter V.) The plan for your course and its weekly and daily activities should include techniques to assess students' work. Will students have a specified amount of time to use teacher feedback to redo work until it meets standards? Will an expectation of your courses include students being able to evaluate their own work and progress? Will you use portfolios as a tool to help students organize their progress and highlight their mastery of standards?

These principles* contribute to your developing an instructional philosophy—your beliefs regarding expectations for students, how best to deliver instruction, and other teaching and learning aspects. You will continue to change and fine-tune your philosophy as your experiences grow and it will be a source of inspiration for your planning choices!

Aim, shoot, score...Setting course goals!

Think about what it takes to score points in sports; a ball gets past a goalie, flies between the uprights or swishes through a net. Regardless of  the sport, you can feel the excitement when those players score. That outcome took practice, and someone planned how the player might best learn to achieve that outcome. If you are to teach your students successfully, you must plan and they must practice. Writing course goals will help you to identify the "big ideas" your students need to learn and to organize instruction over time. You can "piggyback" on these course goals or your state's predetermined POS to articulate and organize all the standards and competencies you are exploring with your students. The goals will reflect not only technical knowledge and skills for your program, but also academic and 21st century skills, such as teamwork and project management (Saavedra & Opfer, 2012).

Examples of course goals are:

- Perform a diagnostic check on brake systems (technical knowledge and skills for Automotive Technology)
- Justify your stance on redesigning landfills in writing (academic knowledge for Natural Resources)
- Document and manage time spent on a marketing project (21st century skills for Business Fundamentals)

Notice that the examples all started with a verb, which suggests an effective way to articulate the expected outcomes. You should have fewer course goals than standards or competencies for your program. These goals become a way to organize the "flow" and "timing" of what you teach and they represent larger, major expectations/targets for learning. These statements can help students get a sense of the overall outcomes for the program and/or course and how they are expected to show their competence. A great sounding board for you is to invite a review and feed-

---

* Principles adapted from Bottoms, G., Pucel, D. & Phillips, I. (1997). Designing Challenging Vocational Courses. Atlanta, GA: Southern Regional Education Board.

back of your program goals from your advisory committee (See Chapter VIII for leveraging this group's expertise.) Experts suggest aiming for about 10-12 goals per course. You also want to make sure your course goals are comprehensive and cover the critical content of your course and the standards represented.

Where the rubber hits the road: Project power!

Although course goals are important and inform the direction of instruction, you also need to decide how to meet those goals and how to design and teach learning activities that support them. An effective vehicle for meeting your course goals can be through the use of projects and major assignments. The use of projects enables you to address multiple standards through a context-driven strategy; students apply knowledge and skills for a real purpose (Pashler, Bain, Bottge, Graesser, Koedinger, McDaniel, & Metcalfe, 2007). Students can also model safety prac-

tices through these types of projects. How do you select these projects and assignments? Think about incorporating the types of activities and projects that someone in your career field would tackle. A project could entail designing something new, assembling and testing a system, troubleshooting a product or solving a community issue. In all cases, these projects provide opportunities for students to take on more ownership of the learning process. For example, teams of Health Science students investigated the spread of infection among a group of student athletes, including scientific aspects of bacterial growth, communicating results via statistics and recommending infection control policies to the district athletic director. The student teams decided on their plan of attack and how they wanted to communicate their results. This project matched several course goals and addressed a number of technical, academic and 21st century skills. In some instances, several assignments will be needed to meet a course goal, such as planning and operating a school-based credit union. Course or program standards are often written in "natural groupings" with performance objectives included. These groupings can inform your project and assignment selections. For example, a Plant Systems pathway under the Agriculture, Food and Natural Resources Career Cluster (States' Career Clusters Initiative, 2008) includes a standard stating, "Examine and apply fundamentals of production and harvesting when producing plants to demonstrate plant management and production techniques" (p 25). This standard, and those grouped with it, suggest that students need experience producing and harvesting plants. This standard can become the focus of a project or unit assignment that includes a multitude of other standards and expectations.

Take time to study your course goals and the standards that relate to your goals; then generate a list of major projects and unit assignments (larger assignments that last several days) and list them in order of importance. Think about a general progression of the skills involved in your project and possible related assignment ideas. Projects that address foundational content—the components that students need first to move forward—are the projects you will address early in the timeframe. These projects may be a bit shorter in scope and/or less complex to allow students to become comfortable with the technical and academic expectations of such assignments.

Move over MapQuest: Charting a course for student success!

Without an understanding of "big picture" planning for your instruction, it is easy to get caught up in the day-to-day activities of a busy classroom. When that happens, your teaching and your students' learning can become hit-and-miss, with skill practice acquired from outside requests such as fixing an uncle's hutch, car or computer. It may seem laborious to contemplate the big ideas, goals, projects and assignments for your entire course, as well as how they fit together over time, but this will become an invaluable "road map" to help you and your students stay on a logical course of learning. One planning tool that helps sequence your learning and identifies gaps in addressing goals is a curriculum map. Curriculum mapping is a process that can help you create a visual reference that shows the interrelationships between your course goals, instructional choices and assessment choices (or how you will know if students get it and if you are improving as a teacher; see Chapters V and VI). A curriculum map can also show where student learning outcomes are taught and assessed within a curriculum. Just as a road map helps you navigate unfamiliar territory and provides landmarks, a curriculum map can offer a similar benefit in guiding you and your students along the expectations and instruction route of your course. Curriculum maps tend to represent a "big picture" timeframe, like a year or semester, but they can also serve to capture monthly or weekly information. These maps can be customized to include what is most helpful for your planning purposes, such as indicating the specific dates within the school year for establishing targets.

In the Toolbox section, a sample curriculum map template is provided. You can change the column headings to accommodate your specific needs. Think about coordinating your curriculum map with your school calendar, noting in-service days, beginning of marking periods, CTSO competition deadlines (see Chapter IV), final exam dates and so forth.

Look at an example entry in a curriculum map and think through the steps you might take to develop one for your program.

In the following *Introduction to Business* map, a column at the far left includes a time notation. In this section you can assign dates or estimated times in terms of days or weeks. Next, you'll want to list the major "units" of study and what focus each has. In this example, the focus is marketing. Finally, you'll want to determine the competencies: the technical, academic and 21st century skills that students will need to master in order to complete the project/unit/assignment. Often these clusters are identified in course/cluster standards lists available through state and district resources, as mentioned in Chapter I. In this particular mapping format, an additional column specifies how students will be assessed. This is where you can record answers to the following question, "What is the evidence that will help you determine whether students have mastered the content?" You will have an opportunity in Chapter V to examine assessment types and functions. Keep in mind that your curriculum map can be updated as you continue planning your course instruction. Your maps will also help you to check whether all of your course standards are being addressed at some point in your course projects and assignments. Like a road map, your map(s) can also be a great reflection tool to review your journey and to make notations on where you altered your plans, sequencing or timing. There is no doubt that good instructional practice takes constant adjustment.

Partial Health Science Curriculum Map

Unit	Unit Title	Course Content Knowledge and Skills			Major Instructional Activities	Assessment
		Technical	Academic	21st Century		
1	Career Exploration, Development and Employability Traits	Health science careers Academic foundation for health science careers Responsibilities of a health career provider Training, education, certification and professional development	Re Determine central ideas. Compare the point of view of two or more authors. Produce clear and coherent writing.	Teamwork Team leadership Positive behaviors and personal qualities Problem solving	Review of teamwork and team building Develop note-taking skills Jigsaw reading of articles	Interper-sonal Skills Paper and Presentation Teamwork Assessment and Self-Evaluation Unit Test

Unit	Unit Title	Course Content Knowledge and Skills			Major Instructional Activities	Assessment
2	Health and Safety Practices	Hazard-free environment

Safety regulations, standards, policies and practices

Occupation-related injuries

Proper body mechanics and ergonomics

State, federal and local work safety, health and environmental regulations

Operation and safety training on equipment | Deliver an oral presentation with visuals.

Use appropriate data sources and geographic tools to analyze public policies. | Workplace safety

Teamwork

Team leadership

Understand national and international public health and safety issues | Anticipation Guide to examine regulations related to health and safety

Safety scenarios | Complete and maintain CPR and Automated External Defibrillation (AED) as well as First Aid certifica-tions |

Curriculum map example from Nancy Headrick, director, Teaching to Lead, NRCCTE and SREB

Planning your projects or instructional units: Questions are the key

CTE programs are a natural place to deliver instruction through authentic projects. Think about all of the opportunities in fields such as automotive technology, HVAC, welding, veterinary sciences, culinary arts and information technology to solve complex problems or create and innovate for the future! Project planning, therefore, can be a value-added skill set for any CTE teacher. Thus far the planning process has included identifying what to teach in your courses, guided by national, state and often industry standards. Using a series of course goals to organize what you teach helps ensure that students are fully prepared for the career field when they master those career goals. Analyze your course goals to: (a) determine the specific technical competencies that students need to learn for project completion; and (b) what supporting academic and 21st century skills will complement students' technical understanding and performance of quality work. This analysis will help you decide how to organize and "chunk" these competencies into project or units/assignments. These can be your building blocks of planning for the course.

Just as raising a new building requires scaffolding to support its construction, planning a project or unit of instruction can benefit from a scaffold, which might be in the form of essential questions. (These are addressed in more detail in Chapter III.) Every project or unit of instruction can embody one or more essential questions that answer the "why" behind the instruction (Hudis & Harris, 2010). *Essential*, or *driving*, questions are open-ended, require deep thought and investigation and focus the project (Curwin, 2015). Often sub-questions stem from

the project's overarching question(s) and these can become the "scaffolding" to help determine the lessons, activities, research focus and other instructional choices. For example, an essential question underlying a criminal justice unit project is, "How do we bring the murderer to justice?" Other questions are essential to this overarching question and help to answer the "why." "How do we investigate a murder?" "How can we be sure you convicted the right person?" "How is a murder suspect convicted?" The scaffolding continues with sub-questions. "How can we tell when the murder occurred?" "What does the crime scene tell us?" "How is DNA evidence used?" "How reliable are witness testimonies?" The questions not only help guide the project or unit instructional strategies and assessments, but they also target and tie the learning standards together (find more detail in Chapter III).

Along with driving or essential questions, a project or unit of instruction can be shaped by using a scenario to invite students into an authentic work role to address a problem. Students will define a problem, investigate possible causes, engage in solving the presented problem and produce a final product or performance that has value outside the classroom. This scenario and the problem-solving process becomes the "backbone" of the instructional activities. An example scenario might be:

> You are a Chef de Cuisine working with your friend who is a restaurant manager; you have decided to be partners in the opening of a new eating establishment in your community. You are tasked with creating a restaurant and an accompanying service style that will contribute to success with what you determine to be your target market. This will include designing a menu based on research of the area, people's needs and wants and what you feel to be your cuisine inspiration.
>
> You must first research the demographics of the area to determine a suitable theme for the restaurant and a possible location; research articles

and data on restaurant trends are important tools. The initial proposal needs to include the comparisons of restaurants in the area and real estate costs. You will need to understand customer's needs and develop menu pricing based on food costs and competitors. Once you have decided your theme, then plan and price your menu. Write a business proposal for your restaurant in which you argue for your design and theme and the other considerations researched. Include the data from your research that support your position. The initial proposal needs to include the comparisons of restaurants in the area, real estate costs, start-up costs and monthly projections of costs and income. As part of the proposal, complete a Food Establishment Permit, using your state's permit requirements as an example. Present your Restaurant Business Proposal to a team of investors from the area looking for a restaurant in which to invest.

The "trifecta" of planning effective project/unit plans is writing a set of objectives that complement your essential questions (guiding, open-ended, underlying 'why' questions) and support your developed scenario. Together,

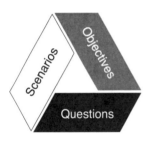

your questions, scenario and a set of project/unit objectives will focus your instruction and help students know the expectations. All of these planning guides/elements should move students toward mastery of course goals and standards. Your aim is to develop objectives that are clear, represent what skills and knowledge are to be learned in the project/unit and are intellectually challenging and are measurable. They guide you and your students directly to what will be assessed. Example objectives are:

- Demonstrate proper use of personal protective equipment when running lab tests (Health Sciences: technical skills)
- Embody professional business demeanor during presentation of a marketing campaign to a customer (Business: 21st century skills)
- Read and analyze information on blueprints of several welded components to determine the overall composition of a fabricated structure (Welding: academic skills)

See the "Tools for your toolbox" section for a unit planning template (that can be used for project planning too!) and suggested development steps.

Lesson planning: Walking is best done one step at a time!

Typically the smallest increment of a teacher's planning responsibilities is to represent what goes on within one class period or day. Now you may be thinking, "Wait a minute, I have unit/project plans. Why do I need a plan for every day?" Good question! As you may have read in a previous handbook, *Your First Year in CTE: 10 Things to Know*, lesson planning helps you avoid all that can ensue when students aren't engaged in their learning and time isn't well spent. A planned lesson also offers the insightful teacher an opportunity to reflect on what worked and what didn't. Lessons are the guide for moving forward with your unit or project plan on a daily basis. Here are some key criteria to keep in mind when developing daily lessons. (There are more in Chapter III.)

Daily Planning

- Focus the lesson so that it connects to the course goals and standards and supports the unit/project.
- Target not only technical skill development, but also related academic learning and 21st century skills.
- Expect students to engage in a complex process of solving a problem or innovation, which requires students to use higher-order thinking skills.
- Incorporate the BSCS (Biological Sciences Curriculum Study, 2015) 5Es into lesson planning: engage, explore, explain, elaborate and evaluate. These are important aspects that encourage active student learning.
- Plan opportunities to provide feedback to students and for students to provide feedback to each other.

Instructional planning is a major function for any conscientious teacher and can make a difference in how students achieve. Knowing your philosophy of what is important, set goals to shoot for, map and organize a flow and timing of student learning, and orchestrate projects, unit assignments and daily lessons that bring out the best in learners! As Confucius says, "Man who does not think and plan long ahead will find trouble right at his door."

Tools for your toolbox

The transition to teaching is exciting and can be a bit overwhelming at first. Considering tools and techniques that maximize student learning and also help structure your classroom time can go a long way to helping meet your teaching goals. A team of field-based teacher educators from West Virginia observe and advise beginning CTE teachers in more than 50 schools. Their chairperson makes the following comment, "We believe the commitment to using research-based instructional planning tools is the best first step toward ensuring consistent, effective and efficient learning experiences for today's students." One of their recent students, new to the CTE teaching profession and preparing to teach cosmetology in a new program, shared her thoughts on the role of long-term planning.

> As a new CTE teacher, I ask myself how do I get from point A to Z without leaving out any information? How do I stay on track to ensure all lessons have been assigned? I found the use of long-term planning tools does just that; they keep me organized and on track. My first step is to refer back to my content skills sets/standards and create a curriculum map. Within this map will be the unit plans that turn into lesson plans. These tools make my life as a teacher a little bit easier.

Once teachers understand that long-term planning is important, they can begin to look at how including projects can enhance the learning experience. These projects can be short- or long-term projects, and they can cover multiple competencies or focus on just one.

We've provided some guidance for establishing a project-based learning experience below.

1. Choose a project or unit assignment focus: Consider and record what students will learn through this project. Include technical, academic and 21st century skills and understandings.
2. Write a scenario that will "set the stage" for what students will investigate and do: Make sure the scenario matches the goals and standards for the project or unit.
3. Determine what the summative assessment (final product, performance or presentation) will be: You can allow students some choice in how to demonstrate their understanding!
4. Outline the formative assessments you will use to check student progress and to provide students with feedback and support: Consider what actions you may take or what resources you can provide to students who may struggle with the project content, or what enrichment options may complement the project work for students who excel.

5. Map out the daily lessons and the activities that will support student progress: Consider including the use of project management skills, such as time-management tools, teamwork strategies and self-assessment techniques.
6. Work with others, if need be, to include literacy and numeracy strategies in your project plan: Keep in mind that the aim is to support the authentic literacy, math and technical skills that are needed to complete the project or unit.

To illustrate this guidance in practice, we've provided an example of a project implementation from an early childhood care and education program. Some of the major units or standards in this program involve: cognitive development, language and communication, community and family relationships and creativity. The CTE teacher developed a project that incorporated these standards by working with other subject teachers to integrate academic knowledge to deliver a project and service to the community. The project involved the CTE students in the childcare and carpentry programs to establish birdhouses throughout the community, and to teach content regarding birds to the preschoolers involved in the early childhood daycare program. A biology teacher assisted her students in creating four learning centers geared for preschoolers. Here are some of the components involved:

1. The interactive modules that biology students delivered to the pre-schoolers involved types of bird feathers, bird nests, bird beaks and bird eggs.
2. The carpentry teacher and his students researched bluebird house designs, drew up plans and then produced 20 wooden bluebird houses.
3. The child care teacher devised a rubric concentrating on measuring gains in the areas of cognitive development, language development and communication and creativity.

This project proved to be not only educational to all students involved, but also fun! Afterward, the biology teacher helped her students to evaluate and reflect on their experience of teaching preschoolers; the childcare teacher gathered feedback from her students and prepped them further for specific assessment. An added value to this integrated activity was that the 20 bluebird houses were placed in the local community in appropriate locations, thus serving as a community service project with a real-world application.

KEY LEARNINGS:

1. Determine your instructional philosophy.
2. Remember to consider your students' learning styles.
3. Curriculum maps can help you and your students look at the big picture.
4. Curriculum maps help you see relationships between 21st century, academic and technical skills.
5. Context-based instruction can be a key ingredient in planning an engaging and innovative project.
6. Remember to reflect on the timing of any long-term projects implemented.
7. Consider using the 5-Es model to ensure student engagement.

RELATED CONTENT THAT MAY BE OF INTEREST:

Bottoms, G., Pucel, D., & Phillips, I. (1997). *Designing Challenging Vocational Courses*. Atlanta, GA: Southern Regional Education Board.

BSCS. (2015). BSCS 5E Instructional Model. Videos and tools available at www.bscs.org/bscs-5e-instructional-model.

Curwin, R. (2015, August 12). Questions Before Answers: What Drives a Great Lesson? *Edutopia Student Engagement* blog. Available at www.edutopia.org/blog/questions-answers-drive-great-lesson-richard-curwin?utm_source=SilverpopMailing&utm_medium=email&utm_campaign=081915%20enews%20ibl%20ngm%20A&utm_content=&utm_term=top1&spMailingID=12166634&spUserID=MjcyNjg1NDgzMDAS1&spJobID=601305544&spReportId=NjAxMzA1NTQ0S0.

Hudis, P. & Harris, K. (2010, March 1). Getting it Right: Performance-Based Curriculum Integration in Small Learning Communities presented at the Educating for Careers Conference, California Center for College and Career, Sacramento, CA. Available at http://2010.ccpc-conference.net/sites/default/files/presentationfiles/Getting%20it%20Right%20-%20Performance-based%20Curriculum%20%28hand-outs%29.pdf.

Pashler, H., Bain, P., Bottge, B., Graesser, A., Koedinger, K., McDaniel, M. and Metcalfe, J. (2007). *Organizing Instruction and Study to Improve Student Learning* (NCER 2007-2004). Washington, DC: National Center for Education Research, Institute of Education Sciences, U.S. Department of Education. Retrieved from http://ncer.ed.gov.

Saavedra, A.R. & Opfer, V.D. (2012, Oct 19). Nine Lessons on How to Teach 21st Century Skills and Knowledge. *The Rand Blog*. Retrieved from www.rand.org/blog/2012/10/nine-lessons-on-how-to-teach-21st-century-skills-and.html.

States' Career Clusters Initiative. (2008). Agriculture, Food and Natural Resources Career Cluster, Plant Systems Pathways Knowledge and Skill Statements. Retrieved from www.careertech.org/sites/default/files/K%26S-CareerPathway-AG-PlantSystems-2008.pdf.

chapter III
How We Deliver CTE Day-by-Day

Lesson planning

It's Thursday, Ms. Neuteach's first day of teacher in-service. Classes for her students begin on Monday. As she takes a deep breath trying to get oriented to her classroom, in walks the CTE director who says, "I want to personally welcome you to Students-R-Stars Technical Center. Glad you found your classroom and are checking things out. I've brought with me some essential materials that you need right away. Here is the course curriculum guide, the state's program of study and required safety standards, a list of media center materials, the instructor's textbook and accompanying teacher software, the student textbook and our format for your daily lesson plans. By the way, you need to hand in your first week of lesson plans to me by Monday. After that, we require one daily lesson plan to be given to an administrator each week prior to teaching that lesson. Any questions? Good. I'll be around if you should need me." And then Ms. Neuteach promptly thinks, "Yikes! I've hardly

Isn't this my stage?

40

had time to look around my classroom and shop area, let alone write a week's worth of lesson plans guided by this huge stack of resources! Guess I can forget about having a personal life this weekend, if I survive."

You may have what is a common concern for many new regular education teachers: a lack of guidance and resources for lesson and unit planning. In a survey of more than 8,000 Teach for America teachers nationwide, 41 percent said that their schools or districts provided them with few or no instructional resources, such as lesson plans, and when classroom materials were available, they were seldom useful (Matthews, 2011). This issue is compounded for CTE teachers because of the specialization of their content. What's a new teacher to do? Fortunately, some schools and states do provide mentor programs for new teachers that can help them survive the first few weeks of school until  they become more familiar with school routines and the resources available to them (Goldrick, Osta, Barlin & Burn, 2012). The importance of having a strong support system for new teachers was discussed in Chapter III in our first handbook, *Your First Year in CTE: 10 Things to Know.*

Ms. Neuteach certainly has a stack of resource materials and guidelines to refer to, but what are the goals, guidelines and industry standards to follow in developing engaging, effective lesson plans for her students? Fortunately, numerous lesson plan formats are readily available online. One potentially helpful resource for new CTE teachers is found at: http://cteteach.cteonline.org/portal/default/Curriculum/Viewer/Curriculum?action=2&view=viewer&cmobjid=856232. Its title is "Part of Lesson Plan: The CTE Online Model Lesson Plan," CTE Online (2011). Emphasis is placed on answering the following key questions when developing lesson plans:

- What is the main idea that you want to teach?
- How can you "hook" (grab the attention of) your students at the start of your lesson and keep them engaged?
- What are the lesson's specific learning objectives (*i.e.,* what should your students be able to do, demonstrate or explain to indicate that they understand the new knowledge or skill)?
- What activities will help your students to achieve the learning objectives?
- How will you assess whether students have met the learning objectives?

This site also provides a helpful checklist to use when developing activities for students. Activities include: the hook, lecture, demonstration/ modeling (of new knowledge or a skill by the teacher), guided practice and independent practice (more on both of these terms later in this chapter), closure activity (to help students summarize the new knowledge/skill and to quickly assess their degree of understanding), checking for understanding (should be done periodically), lab/shop (hands-on work time), group work, projects and formal assessment (grading). More information will be provided about grading in Chapter V in this handbook. A checklist is also provided for several assessment types that include: demonstrating, interviews, journals (hopefully having the additional effect of reinforcing good writing skills), observations, portfolios, projects, rubrics, surveys, teacher-developed tests and writing samples.

An online source for ready-made CTE lesson plans has been created by the Vocational Information Center and can be found at http://khake. com/page94.html. There are other examples of online lesson planning and assessment if your school does not provide a format for you. Don't forget to ask mentors or veteran teachers what works well for their students. Always focus on planning for a variety of engaging, meaningful activities and strategies to optimize students' chances of success. Remember this: it is okay to modify a lesson plan if it is not working or can be improved to better suit the needs of all of your students!

As you work to become more experienced at writing lesson plans, you may want to consult Webb's Depth of Knowledge (DOK) (Webb, 1997), which was developed in the 1990s to help align analysis of curriculum, objectives, standards and assessments. The four categories, in order from the lowest level of thinking to the highest, with basic explanations and examples of verbs, are:

- Recall and Reproduction: to recall a fact, information or procedure; verb examples include arrange, calculate, define, identify, match, measure, recite, illustrate, draw, etc.
- Skill/Concept: to engage a mental process beyond habitual response using information or conceptual knowledge; requires two or more steps; verb examples include apply, categorize, determine cause and effect, estimate, predict, classify, etc.
- Strategic Thinking: requires reasoning, developing a plan or a sequence of steps, some complexity and more than one possible

answer; verb examples include apprise, assess, cite evidence, critique, draw conclusions, investigate, formulate, etc.
- Extended Thinking: requires investigation, complex reasoning, planning, developing and thinking over an extended period of time; verb examples include analyze, apply concepts, compose, connect, design, evaluate, prove, synthesize, etc.

Instructional strategies

After getting some idea about the basics of lesson planning, you'll need to pay attention to which instructional strategies might be used to deliver the lessons effectively to your students. These need to be a part of your lesson plans. In a CTE study (Fletcher, Djajalaksana & Eison, 2012) to determine the most frequently used instructional strategies out of 53 types, the six most frequently used ones were (in order from highest to lower percentage of use):

- Questioning
- Whole-group discussion
- Guided practice
- Interactive lecture
- Self-directed learning
- Problem-based learning

Entire books exist on some of these strategies, but you do not need to be overwhelmed by too much information at this point. The purpose of this chapter will be to provide a basic understanding of each of the top six.

The instructional strategy of *questioning* is based on the teacher providing a lecture-based lesson, asking questions, students answering them and asking questions in return for clarification (Wang & Ong, 2003). This strategy is mostly teacher-led. The main goal is to actively engage students with lower- and higher-level questions during lecturing and to help them link prior knowledge to present knowledge. It also serves to help the teacher to determine the students' understanding of the topic. However, questioning can become very  time-consuming, while encouraging each student to participate, especially in large group settings. Also, shy students may not participate unless called upon, perhaps creating negative feelings. For the questioning instructional strategy to be effective, questions should be worded to suit students' level of understanding of the topic, and teachers must develop a sense of timing, relax and be patient while waiting for students' responses.

The second instructional strategy is *whole-group discussion*. It is similar to questioning, but differs in that it permits students to interact with each other in various ways to help each other's learning, in addition to the teacher's interactions. It is consistent with a more learner-centered style of instruction. It is appealing for auditory learners, but it can be a difficult learning strategy for students who are weak in taking notes during discussions. Teachers may need to teach their students about note-taking skills, and also the importance of being effective in managing and facilitating group discussions with some basic interaction rules in place (Kelly, 2015). Overall, whole-group discussion is an excellent instructional strategy when used in conjunction with other instructional methods.

Practice makes perfect, right? No, not if it is being performed incorrectly! Students must correctly practice the skills an instructor is teaching in order for them to become internalized. In the instructional strategy known as *guided practice*, the instructor first models how to complete a skill, leads the students incrementally through the completion of that skill, monitors the progress of each student toward the successful completion of that skill in a supportive environment, may need to re-teach certain components of the skill during this learning period and provide additional opportunities for students to practice (individually) the new skill in and outside of the classroom (called independent practice). Timely individual feedback must be provided to foster students' progress. Guided practice will be a very effective teaching strategy for CTE educators as they help their students learn numerous new skills to prepare them for employment and/or higher education. A helpful, concise online article on this instructional strategy is "The Importance of Guided Practice in the Classroom" (Herrmann, 2014).

The next instructional strategy, called *interactive lecture*, operates on the principle that the instructor engages students during a lecture by providing an activity (or more) that allows students to practice and apply what they have learned. Students actively participate instead of answering questions only when called upon. The interactive activity should continue to engage them throughout the lesson, allow them to ask questions, to practice the new learning and to provide opportunities to develop critical thinking skills. As with the other instructional methods explained so far, many online resources exist for clarification and examples. A good article is "Interactive Lectures" (Macdonald &Teed, 2015).

In the *self-directed* learning strategy, the learner must possess appropriate independent study skills and a proper attitude for setting up success to include good study habits and a support network at school and at home. The student and instructor must set learning goals, identify resources to be utilized, set timelines to achieve goals, and the instructor must provide feedback and evaluate the students. Even the brightest and most motivated students can be challenged by self-directed learning (Center for Teaching Excellence, 2015). Some CTE instructors have chosen to modify self-directed learning by allowing qualified students in their classes to work independently at times or in small groups to complete a given task. This is known as *project-based learning* and operates similarly to self-directed learning. Project-based learning was previously discussed (Chapter II). Remember that the goals of this type of learning are to help students develop flexible knowledge, effective problem solving skills, self-directed learning, effective collaboration skills and intrinsic motivation (Hmelo-Silver, 2004).

Another instructional model consideration

The BSCS 5Es above references an instructional model developed by the science community, which consists of the following phases: engagement, exploration, explanation, elaboration and evaluation (Bybee, 2009; "The BSCS Instructional Model and 21st Century Skills," paper submitted to The National Academies Board on Science Education). These phases together provide an opportunity for students to better understand knowledge, skills and attitudes and contribute to a teacher's coherent instructional planning. Table 1 summarizes the phases with examples of each phase following.

Table 1. Summary of the BSCS 5Es Instructional Model (Bybee, 2009)

Phase	Summary
Engagement	The teacher or a curriculum task assesses the learners' prior knowledge and helps them become engaged in a new concept through the use of short activities that promote curiosity and elicit prior knowledge. The activity should make connections between past and present learning experiences, expose prior conceptions and organize students' thinking toward the learning outcomes of current activities.
Exploration	Exploration experiences provide students with a common base of activities within which current concepts (i.e., misconceptions), processes and skills are identified and conceptual change is facilitated. Learners may complete lab activities that help them use prior knowledge to generate new ideas, explore questions and possibilities and design and conduct a preliminary investigation.
Explanation	The explanation phase focuses students' attention on a particular aspect of their engagement and exploration experiences and provides opportunities to demonstrate their conceptual understanding, process skills or behaviors. This phase also provides opportunities for teachers to directly introduce a concept, process or skill. Learners explain their understanding of the concept. An explanation from the teacher or the curriculum may guide them toward a deeper understanding, which is a critical part of this phase.

Phase	Summary
Elaboration	Teachers challenge and extend students' conceptual understanding and skills. Through new experiences, the students develop deeper and broader understanding, more information and adequate skills. Students apply their understanding of the concept by conducting additional activities.
Evaluation	The evaluation phase encourages students to assess their understanding and abilities and provides opportunities for teachers to evaluate student progress toward achieving the educational objectives.

Engagement example: Show students a picture related to the lesson and have them free-write as many things as they can about what they can guess about the picture and how it connects to their lives.

Exploration example: Students are encouraged to "get messy" with the concepts through first-hand experiences. Automotive students would tear apart a disc brake and note things they know and don't know.

Explanation example: Students develop an explanation based on their exploration of the disc brakes. The teacher can help identify new vocabulary when students are discussing their findings with each other.

Elaboration example: Students apply what they learn to a new, but related, real-world context. Given a scenario that involves a possible faulty brake issue, students solve a problem and articulate their recommendations. In the CTE environment, this phase can include hands-on practice, in which students construct or create a product or process in teams and/or independently.

Evaluation example: Includes both formative assessment opportunities (checks embedded throughout the lesson) and summative assessment (final task that measures students' achievement of lesson goals). Formative assessments can include oral discussion, journal entry, group report, interview with teacher, etc. Summative assessments may include exit slip, paper and pencil quiz, lab report, etc.

These phases are complemented by an opening and closing of every lesson, whether students are working in the lab or not. Getting students started at the beginning of every day sets a tone for what they are to accomplish. Routines can be established to invite students to jump right into the learning through a thought problem-of-the-day, a story about something related to the objectives and other beginning techniques. In the last few minutes of class, teachers can reiterate what was learned, answer questions and set the stage for what is to come through a sharing discussion, journal/notebook entry, quick student-led review of major points and a report from the student manager or a homework question that they need to investigate.

Teaching styles

Just as there are many forms of lessons, there are many considerations when finding your own " teaching style." (See teaching philosophy in Chapter II.) Think about:

1. What does and does not work for you and your students?
2. Diversify your teaching approach from day to day so as to keep learning "fresh" (not boring) for your students.
3. Remember that teacher-centered approaches have pros and cons as do student-centered approaches.
4. Learn to balance the role of instructor and become a co-learner with your students.
5. Consider using technology to diversify teaching approaches.
6. Try new approaches, keep learning and be flexible (adapted from the University of South Carolina, 2015).

Whatever instruction or learning strategy is chosen for each lesson, remember that learning is not a spectator sport. Students do not learn much just by listening to teachers lecture or by memorizing facts. They must actively engage in what they are learning about in a variety of ways and relate it to what they already know. New information and skills must become internalized and applied to real life if they are going to give meaning to learners and increase the rate of retention for future applications.

Poor Ms. Neuteach. She overhears some teachers in the faculty lounge at lunch discussing "asynchronous or synchronous learning" and thinks, "Huh? Now what the heck do those terms mean? Will I ever feel comfortable with writing lesson plans? I thought I just had to show them the basic skills of my technical area and they would learn it. I never knew so much was involved in teaching kids!" Well, here is a heads-up on those terms. *Asynchronous* learning takes place at one time and is preserved for the learner to access the information whenever the time is most convenient for him or her. However, the student can still interact with peers, provide peer feedback and reflect on the status of his or her personal learning goals and outcomes. Asynchronous learning is considered to be more flexible than synchronous learning. Examples include email, e-courses, online forums, audio and video recordings, even snail mail. Important advantages are that many of the learning tools are free, minimal hardware is needed and opportunities exist for face-to-face interactions and collaborations. The main emphasis of asynchronous learning is that it is designed to be available to the learner when time (and therefore learning) are most convenient and also to be completed at the individual's pace of learning (Higley, 2013).

On the other hand, traditional learning strategies (such as lectures, discussions and lesson presentations) in which the student may be located in a classroom with a teacher at a specific time are appropriate examples of *synchronous* learning. It has been the more widely used style of learning in the past, but asynchronous learning is quickly becoming more popular (Higley, 2013; Thiede, 2012). Both synchronous and asynchronous learning can be integrated to gain the advantages of both.

Essential questions

Developing "essential questions" is a technique that should be employed because it can help guide teachers to consider *what* students need to know and be able to do at the end of the unit, and *how* grade-level work can be assessed. Essential questions communicate to students the crucial points of the curriculum by stressing what they will investigate, probe and research. Essential questions increase the depth of instruction and narrow the focus of a particular lesson. When developing the essential questions, consider the following: What do students really need to know, understand and be able to do at the end of the unit? What knowledge, skills and processes are crucial for mastery?

For a unit that lasts one week or more (as many CTE units do), develop four or five essential questions. Three or four questions should tie directly to the content of the unit, and at least one should connect the content directly to students' lives. Aim for a balance of content and connection. Essential questions should not be answerable with "yes" or "no", but require more in-depth student answers and understanding. Some examples of essential questions are:

- How can understanding food labels help those in the food industry?
- What are the parts of an engine lathe and what is the function of each?
- What safety practices should always be followed in a carpentry shop area and why?

Essential questions should be prominently posted in the classroom and must be easily understood. They send a signal to students to search out answers and use critical thinking skills. They help to guide instruction from the pre-assessment to the completion of the post-assessment. Writing essential questions also leads to self-reflection by teachers during planning and instruction and helps to develop a rigorous unit. The following checklist can be used to determine the strength of essential questions. If the answer to any of the items is "no," one or more essential questions may need to be revised.

Think It Through		
Do the essential questions:	**Yes**	**No**
Address all targeted standards?	☐	☐
Provide direction for teaching and learning?	☐	☐
Connect to the assessments?	☐	☐
Narrow the focus of the lessons to the most important elements?	☐	☐
Encourage higher-order thinking?	☐	☐
Are the essential questions:		
Written in a language students understand?	☐	☐
Written in an open-ended style?	☐	☐
Appropriate to the length of the lesson?	☐	☐
Sequenced for most logical progression?	☐	☐
Distinct and powerful?	☐	☐

Technology

Technology is becoming more visible every day in CTE classes. It can provide teachers with additional strategies to motivate students and to enhance their learning. These can include the use of presentation software (such as PowerPoint or Prezi), classroom computers and laptops (possibly used in conjunction with an electronic, interactive white screen device such as the SmartBoard), classroom response systems (such as "clickers" that are handheld devices used by students to answer questions), online projects and collaboration tools podcasts (that can be used to convey information students need for  initial learning or review), online quizzes, simulations and games, even online courses (Peterson, 2015).

Web 2.0 and other technology tools are making it quicker and easier than ever to create digital portfolios of student work. Digital portfolios showcase student progress, which experts say increases student engagement, promotes a continuing conversation about learning between teachers, parents and students and extends academic lessons beyond school walls. Other tools such as Wikis and blogs allow students to work collaboratively and share their work with a limited or unlimited number of people. The videophone service Skype is also popular with teachers, particularly for allowing their students to connect with peers in other parts of the country or the world (Editorial Projects in Education Research Center, 2011).

How much technology you will utilize to help your students learn will depend on what technology is available within your classroom and what technologies you and your students are willing to learn. You don't need to jump in all at once, but do continue to try new technologies periodically to determine which may be the most effective ones for your students each year. After all, it's your stage!

Tools for your toolbox

According to the Commission on Teacher Credentialing (2008), new teachers should initially:

1. Integrate instruction of related academic skills into their courses.
2. Teach the state-adopted CTE content standards appropriately.
3. Differentiate instruction that takes into consideration cognitive, physical, social and emotional characteristics of adolescents.
4. Pace and adjust instruction based on student assessment.
5. Actively engage students with strategies, activities and materials that are based on different learning theories (e.g., constructivist, socio-cultural, transformational).
6. Utilize instructional strategies appropriate to students of varying abilities in small- and large-group instruction.
7. Allocate instructional time to maximize student achievement.
8. Model correct oral and written language and adjust the complexity of the language to the linguistic abilities of the students.
9. Apply language development strategies (oral, reading and written).
10. Provide individualized instruction when needed for student success.
11. Deliver lessons that are based on instructional goals, student performance objectives, appropriate teaching strategies, safety considerations, relevant classroom materials and assessment data.
12. Plan a unit of instruction consisting of a series of lessons in which at least one concept, skill or topic is taught fully and sequenced effectively.

High Schools That Work (SREB) is recognized as a national school improvement initiative for high schools. The following is one of their sample templates for planning a daily lesson plan. Examples from other sources can be found online as well.

High Schools That Work (HSTW) Unit Planning Template (SREB, 2008)

Unit Title: _____

Course Name: _____

Grade Level: _____

Unit Overview: _____

State/Local Standards: _____

Goals and Essential Questions (Open-ended style, which promotes in-depth investigation):

_____

_____

_____

Post Assessment:

_____

_____

Cycle of Learning Lesson Plan Template (Daily Plan)

Day _____ of _____

Goals/Aims/Essential Questions

_____

_____

_____

_____

State/City Standards for Today's Activities

_____

_____

_____

_____

Anticipated Times * (Add your timeframes)	Sequence of Instruction	Activities Checklist
_____ minutes	Get Started/Do Now	___ Admit slip ___ Post/discuss/copy objectives ___ Write in journal ___ Solve problems ___ Answer questions ___ Pre-assessment ___ Other _____
_____ minutes	Engage/Motivation	___ Display object/picture ___ Demonstrate reaction ___ Model/demonstrate lab ___ Discuss previous experiences ___ Other _____
_____ minutes	Explore/Mini lesson	___ Create lists ___ Brainstorm ___ Build a model ___ Analyze data ___ Evaluate steps ___ Investigate ___ Work problem ___ Lab activity ___ Other _____
_____ minutes	Explain/Mini lesson	___ Lecture with guided notes ___ Student presentations ___ Media presentation ___ Interactive discussion ___ Other _____
_____ minutes	Practice Together/ Application	___ Complete practice problems/labs ___ Use manipulatives ___ Construct graph/timelines ___ Make predictions ___ Collaborative writing ___ Whole group graphic organizers ___ Other _____

Anticipated Times * (Add your timeframes)	Sequence of Instruction	Activities Checklist
_____ minutes	Practice in Teams/ groups/buddy-pairs/ Application	____ Solve similar problems ____ Practice active reading strategies ____ Answer questions ____ Peer review/edit ____ Design other problems/questions/labs ____ Research information ____ Other _____
_____ minutes	Practice Alone/ap-plication	____ Draft writing ____ Answer questions/problems ____ Design/construct other problems/ questions/labs ____ Revise work ____ Design individual investigation/project ____ Other _____
_____ minutes	Evaluate understand-ing (Daily/Weekly/ Post-Assessment)	____ Discussion ____ Open-response question(s) ____ Quiz/test (academic/authentic) ____ Writing sample ____ Individual project/investigation/ presentation ____ Other _____
_____ minutes	Closing Activities/ Summary	____ Assign/explain homework ____ Review major points ____ Answer questions ____ Student reflection activity ____ Exit slip ____ Other _____
_____ As Needed	Enrichment/Exten-sion/Re-teaching/ Accommodation(s)	____ Review ____ Practice ____ Reading ____ Tutoring ____ Individual assignment ____ Other _____

The following daily sequence checklist can assist the teacher in developing lesson plans. It provides a pre-teaching strategy for planning plus what is expected during the lesson. However, it could also be used for reflection after the lesson has been taught to determine if revisions are needed for the next time it is taught.

Daily Sequence Checklist
Ask these questions about the daily plan.

Day # _____ **Standards/Objectives/Readiness Indicators:**	**Yes**	**No**
Targets and helps students achieve specific district/state standard/ standards?	❐	❐
Identified and posted for students to see?	❐	❐
Stated in terms of what the student knows, understands and applies?	❐	❐
Builds on previous learning?	❐	❐
Includes one habit of success?	❐	❐
Includes identified literacy strategies?	❐	❐
Get Started—Bell Ringer, Do Now, Problem of the Day, etc.	**Yes**	**No**
Visible to students as they enter the classroom?	❐	❐
Eliminates wasted time with clear directions?	❐	❐
Includes student accountability for finishing in allotted time?	❐	❐
Establishes expectations of behavior for getting started without teacher support?	❐	❐
Supports the standards?	❐	❐
Self-directing, challenging, but does not frustrate students?	❐	❐
Sets the stage and establishes a mood for learning?	❐	❐
Fits the age and activity level of the students?	❐	❐
Engage	**Yes**	**No**
Hooks the attention/interest of the students?	❐	❐
Sets the stage and establishes the purpose for learning?	❐	❐
Connects to and supports the Standards and the Get Started activity?	❐	❐
Uses higher-order thinking questions to establish learning?	❐	❐
Matches the age, activity levels and learning styles of the students?	❐	❐
Explore	**Yes**	**No**
Builds students' experiences through discovery?	❐	❐
Introduces and builds vocabulary?	❐	❐
Supports and extends the standards and the engagement activity?	❐	❐

	Yes	No
Includes a majority of higher-order questions?	☐	☐
Focuses students on the content, rather than the flash appeal?	☐	☐
Explain	**Yes**	**No**
Delivers content in the most appropriate (research-based) delivery format?	☐	☐
Focuses on one of the four types of advance organizers: expository, narrative, skimming or graphic?	☐	☐
Ensures that students organize information?	☐	☐
Uses a research-based format for note-taking, such as teacher-prepared, interactive or combination notes?	☐	☐
Includes print or broadcast media with guide, discussion and other types of presentations?	☐	☐
Includes frequent checks for understanding throughout the process of explanation/direct instruction?	☐	☐
Utilizes a variety of visuals to focus on answers, such as "thumbs up," group sampling, quick informal pair-shares, etc., that maximize active participation?	☐	☐
Scripts questions into the lecture/explanation so that all levels of Bloom's/Anderson's cognitive taxonomy are included?	☐	☐
Focuses the cues and questions on what is important as opposed to the unusual?	☐	☐
Focuses on higher-level questions?	☐	☐
Connects standards to the real world and helps students "make sense" of the content?	☐	☐
Includes short- and long-term student accountability?	☐	☐
Helps target and build on one habit of success?	☐	☐
Includes examples to model new content and skills?	☐	☐
Practice Together	**Yes**	**No**
Includes rigorous, minds-on, hands-on practice?	☐	☐
Allows teacher to monitor and support during this practice?	☐	☐
Addresses multiple learning styles? Addresses multiple learner profiles (learning styles, multiple intelligences, gender, etc.)?	☐	☐
Includes content that continues to scaffold and spiral?	☐	☐
Ensures students' engagement with note-taking, etc.?	☐	☐
Requires students to collect individual information during whole-group practice?	☐	☐
Sets students up to take the lead in learning and provide additional examples?	☐	☐
Focuses practice on specific aspect(s) of a complex skill or process?	☐	☐
Allows for student success?	☐	☐

Practice in Teams/Groups/Buddy-Pairs	Yes	No
Uses the most appropriate grouping method for this content: buddy-pairs, small or cooperative groups?	☐	☐
Includes similar, but varied problems based on standards?	☐	☐
Requires less teacher-directed support and more student-directed practice?	☐	☐
Allows teacher to monitor and provide specific extra help?	☐	☐
Incorporates the identified habit of success?	☐	☐
Incorporates Literacy Strategies?	☐	☐
Practice Alone	**Yes**	**No**
Helps students transfer knowledge gained during the previous practice strategies to new problems and situations?	☐	☐
Includes appropriate number of problems or examples?	☐	☐
Supports individual accountability through notebooks, reports, etc.?	☐	☐
Includes distributive practice spread out over time so that students maintain and deepen content knowledge and skills?	☐	☐
Evaluate Understanding	**Yes**	**No**
Utilizes most appropriate assessment method?	☐	☐
Uses a combination of written and oral questioning?	☐	☐
Allows for feedback that can drive future instruction?	☐	☐
Provides for demonstration of partial or complete mastery of the content?	☐	☐
Allows for re-teaching, if mastery is not achieved?	☐	☐
Identifies specifics of students needing extra help?	☐	☐
Specifies if extra help is needed for process, skills or content?	☐	☐
Closing Activities	**Yes**	**No**
Cements students' understanding of the content?	☐	☐
Maintains control until the end of class?	☐	☐
Answers questions and clarifies instructions?	☐	☐
Sets up next day's instruction?	☐	☐
Explains the purpose and outcome for homework (practice, preparation for new learning, elaborate on new information)?	☐	☐
Provides a way for all students to participate in closure?	☐	☐
Includes a way for all students to verbalize what the learning was (whip-around, popcorn, outcome sentences, exit tickets, reflection journal, etc.)	☐	☐

Enrichment/Extension	Yes	No
Pushes students to go beyond proficient or advanced-level mastery of the content?	❒	❒
Encourages students to demonstrate higher levels of cognition: application, analysis, synthesis, etc.?	❒	❒
Allows teacher to continue with other students, if necessary?	❒	❒
Differentiates homework or provides student choice during homework?	❒	❒
Accommodation(s)/Re-teaching	**Yes**	**No**
Addresses identified skills for students who need extra help or extra time?	❒	❒
Connects to and supports standards?	❒	❒
Addresses weaknesses identified on preassessments?	❒	❒
Fits needs for multiple levels of extra help?	❒	❒
Allows teacher to continue with other students, if necessary?	❒	❒
Fits fairly into the grading system?	❒	❒

KEY LEARNINGS:

1. Good lesson planning considers many variables.
2. Lesson plans need to be flexible and revised based on student interaction.
3. Consider the hierarchy of recall, concept, strategic thinking and extended thinking.
4. Numerous instructional strategies are available to deliver lessons.
5. Develop your own teaching style, but keep it fresh.
6. Essential questions help to guide the learner.
7. Consider how technology might enhance your lesson.

RELATED CONTENT THAT MAY BE OF INTEREST:

ACTE. (2015) Lesson Plan Search. *Educator Resources*. Available at www.acteonline.org/lessonPlanSearch.aspx?id=131.

Center for Teaching Excellence (2015). *Teaching Styles: 7 Things to Consider About Teaching Styles*. University of South Carolina. Available at www.sc.edu/cte/guide/teachingstyles/.

CTE Online. (2011). *CTE Online Lesson Plan Template—Word Version*. Available at http://cteteach.cteonline.org/portal/default/Resources/Viewer/ResourceViewer?action=2&resid=389264.

Fletcher Jr., E.C., Djajalaksana, Y., & Eison, J. (2012). Instructional Strategy Use of Faculty in Career and Technical Education. *Journal of Career and Technical Education, 27* (2, winter), 69-83. Available at http://files.eric.ed.gov/fulltext/EJ995896.pdf.

Goldrick, L., Osta, D., Barlin, D. & Burn, J. (2012, February). *Review of State Policies of Teacher Induction*. Santa Cruz, CA: New Teacher Center. Available at www.newteachercenter.org/sites/default/files/ntc/main/resources/brf-ntc-policy-state-teacher-induction.pdf.

Herrmann, E. (2014, February 12). The Importance of Guided Practice in the Classroom. *Multi Briefs: Exclusive.* Available at http://exclusive.multibriefs.com/content/the-importance-of-guided-practice-in-the-classroom/education.

RELATED CONTENT THAT MAY BE OF INTEREST, continued:

Higley, M. (2013, October 13). Benefits of Synchronous and Asynchronous e-Learning Industry. Available at http://elearningindustry.com/benefits-of-synchronous-and-asynchronous-e-learning.

Hmelo-Silver, C. (2004). Problem-based learning: What and How Do Students Learn? *Education Psychology Review, 16* (3), 235-266. Available at http://link.springer.com/article/10.1023%2FB%3AEDPR.0000034022.16470.f3.

Kelly, M. (2015). Whole Group Discussion Pros and Cons. *About Education.* Available at http://712educators.about.com/od/lessonplans/p/discussions.htm.

Kentucky Tech Curriculum. (2015). Available at www.kytechcurriculum.org/lp_Main.asp.

Macdonald, H., & Teed, R.; updated by Hoyt, G., Imazeki, J., Millis, B., &Vazquez-Cognet, J. (2015, May 28). Interactive Lectures. *Pedagogy in Action.* Available at http://serc.carleton.edu/sp/library/interactive//index.html.

Peterson, D. (2015). What is the Difference Between Asynchronous and Synchronous Learning? *About Education.* Available at http://adulted.about.com/od/glossary/g/Asynchronous-Learning.htm.

Southern Region Education Board (SREB). (2008). *Planning for Improved Student Achievement.* Atlanta, GA: Author. Available at http://publications.sreb.org/2008/08V05_SBU_Intro.pdf.

Thiede, R. (2012). Best Practices with Online Courses. *U.S.-China Education Review* A 2, 135-141. ERIC Number: ED532176. Available at http://files.eric.ed.gov/fulltext/ED532176.pdf.

Utah Education Network. *K-12 Core Lesson Plans.* Available at www.uen.org/k12educator/corelessonplans.shtml.

Vocational Information Center. (2012, August 26). *Career and Technical Education Web Resources.* Available at www.khake.com/.

Wang, C. & Ong, G. (2003, February). Questioning Techniques for Active Learning. *Ideas on Teaching.* Available at www.cdtl.nus.edu.sg/ideas/iot2.htm.

Webb, N. L. (1997). *Criteria for Alignment of Expectations and Assessments in Mathematics and Science Education.* Council of Chief State School Officers and National Institute for Science Education Research Monograph No. 6. Madison, WI: University of Wisconsin. Available at http://facstaff.wcer.wisc.edu/normw/WEBBMonograph6criteria.pdf.

chapter IV
Using CTSOs to Enhance Your Content

Career technical student organizations (CTSOs) and your program

Flowers and bees. Batman and Robin. Locks and keys. Macaroni and cheese. Socks and shoes. Peanut butter and jelly. Some things in life just go well together. They bring out the best in each other, and together make a terrific combination! That's how CTSOs can affect your CTE program—the perfect partner for providing opportunities for your students to develop as professional leaders. This chapter provides information and suggestions on the exciting world of student organizations and how they can enhance and complement your program!

The best complement for your classroom!

When you consider your role as a CTE teacher and the challenge of preparing students for the future, it can be a bit overwhelming. Luckily, there are some really great resources

What things go great together?

that will help you with your professional charge. All teachers have a shared goal to help develop students for future success. The moving target in this picture may be figuring out what it takes to be successful in tomorrow's workforce. Students not only need to acquire technical and academic skills and knowledge, they can also benefit from developing employability and leadership skills. This combined set of skills will help your students advance and navigate their professional career trajectory. This is where CTSOs become a valuable resource and a super complement to the teaching and learning in your program and institution.

Just as technical skills are best learned through a combination of theory and application, employability and leadership skills are learned the same way. Students need opportunities to develop as future leaders, active members of a community and professionals in their work lives (ACTE, 2006). CTSOs are the "playing field" to practice and hone these complementary skills. For a new teacher, it can be exciting to learn that you alone don't have to create these professional networks and hands-on opportunities for your students—these networks exist already and they are a win-win for both you and your students!

Students' school experience can be enhanced by involvement in activities like sports, band, belonging to a theatre group or an outside-of-school organization like scouting or the Jaycees. In fact, employers who are hiring are often interested in students' participation in extracurricular activities and whether they have taken on leadership roles or other responsibilities. Why, then, would CTE students and teachers be interested in CTSOs? How are these organizations different from the many extracurricular activities available to students? Good question! CTSOs are specifically designed to support students in CTE programs by providing them with career-focused networks that offer opportunities to develop their skills, giving them labor market advantage. CTSOs are considered "co-curricular" or "inside the curriculum" and they address course standards and expectations alongside your technical curriculum and instruction (National Coordinating Council for Career and Technical Student Organizations [NCC-CTSO], 2015). The opportunities and activities offered through CTSOs also have a benefit similar to extracurricular activities of sports, band, etc. they offer students an opportunity to belong to a positive, career-supporting network.

CTSOs provide students an opportunity to make a positive choice. They can serve as a strong influence for students who may be without family guidance and/or without meaningful ways to spend their time. Through CTSOs, students are part of something larger, not only locally, but also at the state and national levels as they connect with a network of career-focused professionals. The programs offer leadership development, skill development and benchmarking, motivation and recognition for both secondary and postsecondary CTE students. The CTSO curriculum-based activities and experiences become tools for you to help students gain career, leadership and personal skills. Many CTE teachers find it useful to include involvement in a CTSO as a program requirement to address those important skill sets.

Benefits and backing!

So, you might ask yourself, "How large are these organizations? How many are there? Is there an organization that would serve my students? Does

participation in a CTSO benefit students?" As a new CTE teacher, it is comforting to know that CTSOs have a rich and positive history and are considered a value-added aspect of any CTE program.

A national coordinating council for CTSOs, NCC-CTSO, which is a coalition of national CTSOs, serves CTE students and teachers across the country and relates to one or more of the 16 career clusters identified in the National Career Clusters Framework (discussed in Chapter I). CTSOs are comprised of 11 not-for-profit organizations and are specifically authorized by the United States Congress in the Carl D. Perkins Career and Technical Education Act of 2006 (Fiscus & Hyslop, 2008). A recent study conducted by the National Research Center for Career and Technical Education (NRCCTE) found that participation in a CTSO offers beneficial effects and the benefits increase as participation increases (Alfeld, Stone, Aragon, Hansen, Zirkle, Connors, Spindler, Romine, & Woo, 2007). Specifically:

- Students who participate in CTSOs demonstrate higher levels of academic engagement and motivation, civic engagement, career self-efficacy and employability skills than other students.
- Participating in leadership and professional development activities in a CTSO raises students' educational aspirations.

The NCC-CTSO suggests that, with more than two million student members combined, the 11 CTSO organizations have a positive impact on students' overall college and career readiness. For a new CTE teacher who wants to provide an effective combination of learning opportunities and experiences, your students' participation in a CTSO is a great complement to your program!

Is there a CTSO for my students?

Yes! The Office of Career, Technical and Adult Education (OCTAE), U.S. Department of Education (www2.ed.gov/about/offices/list/ovae/pi/cte/vso. html), recognizes the following 11 CTSOs and provides the following information:

Business Professionals of America (bpa.org)

Business Professionals of America has a history as a student organization that contributes to the preparation of a world-class workforce through the advancement of leadership, citizenship, academic and technological skills for students at the secondary and the postsecondary levels. Through co-curricular programs and services, members of Business Professionals of America compete in demonstrations of their business technology skills, develop their professional and leadership skills, network with one another and professionals across the nation and get involved in the betterment of their community through service projects.

DECA (deca.org)

DECA, a national association of marketing education students, provides members and teachers with educational and leadership development activities to supplement classroom instruction.

Future Business Leaders of America-Phi Beta Lambda (fbla-pbl.org)

FBLA-PBL is a dynamic organization of young people preparing for success as leaders in our businesses, government and communities. This site was created to help current and prospective FBLA-PBL members find information about the association, its programs, services and members.

Educators Rising (https://educatorsrising.org)

Educators Rising, sponsored by Phi Delta Kappa International, is a student organization that provides students interested in education-related careers with activities and materials that help them explore the teaching profession in a variety of ways. Educators Rising is the former Future Educators Association and helps students develop the skills and strong leadership traits that are found in highly qualified educators, and significantly contributes to the development of the next generation of great educators.

Family, Career and Community Leaders of America (fcclainc.org)

Family, Career and Community Leaders of America (FCCLA) is a national CTSO that provides personal growth, leadership development and career preparation opportunities for students in family and consumer sciences education. By exploring many roles—that of family member, wage earner and community leader—members develop skills for life through: character development, creative and critical thinking, interpersonal communication, practical knowledge and career preparation.

Health Occupations Students of America (hosa.org)

Health Occupations Students of America (HOSA) is a national student organization with a two-fold mission to promote career opportunities in the health care industry and to enhance the delivery of quality health care to all people. HOSA's goal is to encourage all health care instructors and students to join and be actively involved in the HOE-HOSA Partnership.

National FFA Organization (ffa.org)

FFA's mission is to make a positive difference in the lives of students by developing their potential for leadership, personal growth and career success through agricultural education.

National Postsecondary Agricultural Student Organization (nationalpas.org)

The National Postsecondary Agricultural Student Organization (PAS) is an organization associated with agriculture/agribusiness and natural resources courses offered at approved postsecondary institutions granting associate degrees or vocational diplomas and/or certificates.

National Young Farmer Educational Association (nyfea.org)

National Young Farmer Educational Association is the official adult student organization for agricultural education as recognized by the United States Department of Education. With the goal of being America's Association for Educating Agricultural Leaders, the association features leadership training, agricultural career education and community service opportunities.

SkillsUSA (skillsusa.org)

SkillsUSA is a national organization serving high school and college students and professional members who are enrolled in technical, skilled and service occupations, including health occupations.

Technology Student Association (tsaweb.org)

The Technology Student Association (TSA) is the only student organization devoted exclusively to the needs of technology education students who are presently enrolled in, or have completed, technology education courses.

The membership philosophy of CTSOs is to provide an organization that is inclusive, not exclusive. Even though the organizations include competitive events to cultivate and recognize technical and 21st century skills, all students can benefit from becoming members. There are many examples of success stories whereby students who normally would not have stepped into a leadership role, joined in making decisions, took risks and pursued their dreams and did so because of joining a student organization (Alfeld, Stone et al., 2007). The next section outlines some "how to" techniques for consideration and encourages their integration into your daily classroom practices. By using these techniques you will give students opportunities to better themselves, peers, program, school and community.

Leadership nuts and bolts: So how does a CTSO work?

Even though unique differences exist between student organizations beyond career focus, a set of programmatic opportunities is common to all. These opportunities make up a program of learning that encompasses organizational objectives and the goals for members. First, consider how leadership skills are developed. Students need an opportunity not only to learn about leadership skills but also to put them into action. The CTSOs provide teachers and schools with a platform of activities, information and resources all designed to help students to mature as leaders in their chosen profession. ACTE also has many resources on its website http://www.acteonline.org/general.aspx?id=2215. Students organize themselves into chapters, with bylaws and protocols, governed by the state and national organization constitutions (Fiscus & Hyslop, 2008). Students meet regularly at scheduled meetings and teachers, in the role of advisor, sponsor the chapters/organization. Student committees work on projects and activities to accomplish goals. Chapters may include the following as part of their work/functions:

- Electing and training officers: Students can use this opportunity to develop their own leadership philosophy and platform for how to serve their peers, the school and their communities. Often, classrooms or schools will hold a formal election and students will campaign, provide information on their qualifications, give speeches and participate in the electoral process. Schools and/or state associations may offer specialized training for newly elected officers. (Skills in action: This is a great opportunity for students to reflect on their strengths as leaders, practice oral communications, work with other students—perhaps a campaign manager and team of supporters—and determine what the greatest needs are for their classroom, the school and their community.)

- Organizing membership: Current members and officers can hold membership drives, develop ways to communicate benefits and expectations to prospective members and manage membership data. (Skills in action: Recruiting for their chapter, students can also apply these same skills to recruiting for their class/program.)

- Holding chapter meetings: Students develop an agenda, become familiar with Roberts Rules of Order (Kennedy, 1997) and par-liamentary procedure, engage the committee's members, learn how to work with each other, and leverage this knowledge to build a successful chapter. (Skills in action: Most workplaces, whether formal or informal, hold meetings during which decisions that affect the workplace need to be made. Students can learn these skills through their CTSO efforts and also use the same procedures and skills to manage decisions about their program and school.)

- Professional development (PD): Students can help organize PD opportunities for a class such as guest speakers, specialized training, peer instruction and leadership events. Chapters can also sponsor and support such events for their school and community (Skills in action: PD can be a great extension of your program goals and students will become more invested if they can assist with organizing the PD. For example, student leaders at a Midwest career center helped sponsor and orchestrate a school-wide interviewing day in which business and industry representatives participated in mock job interviews related to each CTE program.)

- Community Service: Tapping into students' affective domain and intrinsic motivations, these opportunities expand students' awareness of needs and commitment to serve others. Chapters plan, organize and provide service to their communities in various and creative ways. (Skills in action: From organizational skills to public relations, students can thrive when asked to help address needs and problems in their communities. A group of HOSA students created an "adult prom" experience for residents at an assisted-care facility they were visiting during their field experience. They decorated the room, arranged music, prom clothing, props, activities, queen and king photo-shoots, and worked with the nursing/management staff to pull it all together for the appreciative residents.)

- Managing local competitive events: Students have opportunities to compete at local, state and national levels in technical and leadership events. Competitions are an exciting, fulfilling and sometimes tricky arena to navigate. More on these will be discussed in the next section of this chapter. (Skills in action: Competitive events are not only an opportunity for students to measure and benchmark their technical preparedness, but also a chance for teachers to get a sense of what standards and priorities are represented by the events. Local competitions can become a performance assessment for all students as well as help determine who will represent your class/chapter in the competitive arena.)

- Fundraising: A transferrable skill set in many ways, chapters can experience raising and managing funds and resources to support their program of work. Fundraising may range from selling third-party goods to holding events and charging admission (think car show and yard sale at your center!), to approaching business partners for support on a specific project.

You can also check each CTSO's website to find helpful information and advice on incorporating program-of-work elements. Other chapters may include relations with the public or business and industry, job-shadowing or other programmatic aspects that help to move their work forward, and serve their classroom/program/school goals. The program of work can truly be customized to serve the chapter and can support the instructional goals of the program. Enter the advisor...

In the world of CTSOs, students are empowered to lead and teachers take on the role of advisors. How does this work? Teachers still play a critical role in the learning process and develop ways to guide students, ask questions and become a sounding board for ideas. Where to start? A first step would be to get familiar with your CTSO and all that it has to offer. Each national organization has a membership department that can provide you with a packet of information on how to get started. Each organization's website also has links to resources. Another great source of assistance is a state director or advisor. Most states have specialists at the state department of education who specialize in CTSOs. Your colleagues can probably help you join in the fun too!

Competitive events: Leveraging the honor and the experience

In the world of CTSOs, it may be worth discussing the impact of competitive events (Threeton, Ewing, & Clark, 2010). These are a mainstay of student organizations and are a great source of inspiration, recognition, accomplishment, joy, tears, frustration and more. The bottom line is that student organizations are about leadership development for all CTE students. Competitive events tend to be the most anticipated and most well-known aspect of most chapter activities and can provide huge and exciting opportunities and recognition for students. These events, if misused, can also perpetuate a "selective approach" to membership and involvement. It is worth considering the following ground rules when planning what role competitive events will play in your CTSO involvement:

- Competitive events are designed to begin at the "local level" or school-based level. Therefore, a great way to involve all students is to hold a local competition as part of your program's instruction so all students can benchmark their progress and experience a competitive atmosphere. Advisory committee members can be helpful as judges to provide specific industry-related feedback for technical events.
  - Your local events should mirror the technical standards and objectives for the state- and national-level events. Your local competitions can then prepare potential competitors to represent your school while offering everyone the experience. Each CTSO website has information and guidance on its respective events.
  - Local competitions should also include leadership events to promote academic and 21st century skills and involve more students.
  - Setting a standard of proficiency through your local competition helps to ensure that students who wish to participate beyond the local level are prepared to do so. It is difficult for students, and often a negative experience, to compete against fellow students when they are not fully prepared to participate in state events.
- Competition may not be the activity that interests all students. Some are not competitive by nature, so encouraging your officers and members to think creatively about other avenues for recognition and showcasing achievement can open doors for other noncompetitive members. Opportunities may even include roles that

support the competitive events or participants, such as a media manager, or events planner who helps orchestrate the behind-the-scenes activities of competitions. Other chapter members may find satisfaction in creating the competition's public-relations materials or writing articles for the local news. The key to a healthy, active chapter is balance in the program of work so there are many different opportunities for students to contribute and shine!

- Competition can provide advisors and school leaders an opportunity to promote "the art of winning and losing." Competition can often result in teachable moments on not only how to handle losing, but also winning. When stakes are high, the reactions of adults in the school provide models for behavior. The reactions to fairness of criteria, judgment from others, jumping to conclusions without proper investigation and consistency of evaluators are all possible areas to address. Keeping an important focus on learning and growth as the purpose of competitive events helps fuel a positive perspective.

It's hard work, but it's worth it!

The benefit of really connecting with your students and providing them opportunities for growth and reflection as bourgeoning leaders in their field can really justify the work of being an advisor. Schools that approach CTSO advisor involvement as a shared responsibility can often support a well-rounded program of work. CTSOs also provide teachers with a great professional network. You become part of a network of caring teachers who really want their students to be successful. These teachers can be a great classroom resource for you as you deal with curriculum instruction and school challenges.

CTSOs are also a great source of recognition. Students and teachers have an opportunity to join a national network that represents a specific technical area. Business and industry representatives partner with these organizations to provide students with scholarships and recognition opportunities. CTSOs can also act as a forum to connect teachers with opportunities for industry donations or grants to support program goals.

Many CTSOs also offer students formal professional development programs that provide recognition by levels of achievement based on demonstration of learning (Association for Career Technical Education, 2011). The basis for this recognition can be organizational knowledge, employability skills or leadership. These programs can be quite extensive and demonstrate a student's multi-year progression through a CTE program. These and the numerous recognition opportunities presented through a rich, engaging program of work complement a high-quality CTE program. So, when someone says, "Isn't it work to be a CTSO advisor?" You can answer, "Yes... and it's worth it!"

Tools for your toolbox

It is amazing to ask advisors of CTSOs about their experiences; you'll find many with a deep level of commitment to their organization. They speak of the opportunities their students have had, how they may themselves have been a member when they were in school and they often mention lifelong friendships that grew from their involvement. One of the current CTSO executive directors started his educational journey as a welding student in a small rural school. When interviewed about his role now, he said he firmly believes that getting involved in CTE and joining his CTSO at school set a course for his successful future.

Not surprisingly, when you reach out to teachers who are involved with their CTSOs, you'll find a really committed, passionate and student-centered group! What matters to this group is motivating their students. CTSOs provide opportunities to bring traits such as value, success, positive relationships and individual growth to life. The role of advisor also helps shape a teacher's philosophy of what matters in education and how teachers see themselves in this important work. A new-to-teaching agriculture education teacher and FFA advisor, from West Virginia, puts it this way:

> I have one biological child, but I frequently find myself telling people about all of "my kids". As an FFA Advisor, I have been given the unique opportunity to make students family. Once they are part of my FFA family, it is my responsibility to help them identify their talents, teach them what it means to serve their community and to help them become useful citizens. I encourage and believe in them, even when they don't believe in themselves. With these responsibilities comes the reward of knowing you have made a difference in children's lives. The greatest feeling as a teacher and FFA Advisor comes when a student has reached their potential or goal and they tell you, "I am here, because you cared."

Often, teachers who were involved in a CTSO as students carry that experience and commitment to leadership development into their role as a teacher. A CTE teacher in Rhode Island began her long-running commitment to SkillsUSA when she was a student by serving as a state officer. When she began her teaching career, she jumped into being an advisor after just one year of teaching! When she received the honor of being named the 2011 Advisor of the Year in her state, she shared her experiences about her CTSO's competitive events:

> In my classroom, competing in SkillsUSA is not only the most exciting event for our school year, but it has also proven to be the driving force

for the students' commitment to quality workmanship, professionalism and rigor. I watch students come together as teams in such competitions as esthetics and nail care and I see the team effort on the individual competitions such as cosmetology and job skill demonstration. The students spend many hours helping each other improve. As a SkillsUSA Advisor, I get to work with all the different career areas and see how each of them have to 'pull out all the stops' to be the very best they can be.

My life has been forever changed by SkillsUSA because as an adult who has gone to the national competitions many times with students from our school, I see what a life-changing experience it can be. Each step the students take while involved, whether they win or not, helps them grow and commit to their school and community through this organization. They commit to good workmanship, professionalism and ethics.

The authors believe that a foundation is created when we encourage our students to participate in programs like SkillsUSA. It reinforces to those students that their participation helps build the future workforce of our country.

We thought that this reflection of a new CTE precision machining teacher from Pennsylvania would also help illustrate the benefits of CTSO participation.

I was hired as the new CTE teacher half-way through a school year. Coming into a teaching position mid-stream was probably the hardest thing I have ever had to do. Having no formal training in the teaching profession, I relied on my experience in the trade; I took the plunge to become a CTE teacher. Managing a classroom full of 10th, 11th and 12th grade students, making worksheets, preparing tests and coming up with shop projects soon became overwhelming. Not to mention the writing of lesson plans, making presentations, repairing machinery and purchasing tooling and supplies. I soon started wondering what had I gotten myself into. After my first year and a half, though, I can look back and see that I have a good foundation in place and things are running much more smoothly.

One of the reasons becoming a CTE teacher was hard was a lack of meaningful student feedback. There seemed to be no real signs of whether I was doing a good job or not. Did my students really understand the information I was giving them? Did they understand the importance of the particular topics or were they just breathing and looking into space?

I had the opportunity to send three students to the state-level SkillsUSA competitions. Two students earned 1st place and one student earned 4th place. Out of those three students, one student was eligible to move on to the national competition where he captured 2nd place. This was the point when I had to sit back and say 'yes, there's my feedback, I must have done something right!' That was justification to me that I had continued where

71

the last instructor left off and filled in the missing pieces for the students to compete well enough to place in a competitive skills event. Another piece of justification came after a phone call from my 2nd place national winner. In that phone conversation, the student told me if he had been in my class for the full three years he felt he could have won the competition.

A senior instructor told me shortly after I was hired as a teacher that after three years, teaching will become easier. I can already see that happening. I said earlier that I felt that I have a good foundation built. I didn't say I have the house built yet. Within the next two years, I hope to finish the house and have a good curriculum built, but homes always seem to need to be remodeled and to have improvements made. The same holds true for CTE. You're never really done, and your students and their field of interest are ever-changing.

The decision to become a CTE teacher was not an easy one, but it has been enjoyable to witness the students grow and to know I've helped put qualified people into industry. I can definitely see myself continuing down this career path and I hope that my participation in CTSOs continue to provide benefits to both me and my students.

KEY LEARNINGS:

1. Career Technical Student Organizations (CTSOs) are a value-added complement to CTE classrooms/programs.
2. Increased CTSO participation equals increases in readiness for college and careers.
3. CTSOs offer students leadership and employability skills through interactive participation in local, state and national networks.
4. There are eleven nationally recognized CTSOs.
5. Teachers serve in an advisory role in CTSO chapters.
6. Competitive events are an exciting and rewarding aspect of a CTSO.
7. CTSOs are a valuable professional network for teachers.

RELATED CONTENT THAT MAY BE OF INTEREST:

Alfeld, C., Stone, J. R., Aragon, S. R., Hansen, D. M., Zirkle, C., Connors, J., Spindler, M, Romine, R. & Woo, H. (2007). *Looking Inside the Black Box: The Value Added by Career and Technical Student Organizations to Students' High School Experience*. St. Paul, MN: National Research Center for Career and Technical Education, University of Minnesota. Available at www.nrccte.org/sites/default/files/publication-files/looking_inside_the_black_box.pdf.

ACTE factsheets. Available at www.acteonline.org/factsheets/#. Vc32ipfvfh4.

Association for Career and Technical Education. (2006). Reinventing the American High School for the 21st Century: Strengthening a New Vision for the American High School Through the Experiences and Resources of Career and Technical Education. A Position

Paper. Alexandria, VA: Author. Available at www.acteonline.org/uploadedFiles/Assets_and_Documents/Global/files/Reinventing_American_High_School.pdf.

Association for Career Technical Education. (2011, June). Expanding Career Readiness Through Career Technical Student Organizations. Alexandria, VA: Author. Available at www.acteonline.org/WorkArea/DownloadAsset.aspx?id=2116.

Association for Career Technical Education. CTE Clearinghouse: Career and Technical Student Organizations. Available at www.acteonline.org/general.aspx?id=2215#.Vc35bJfvfh4.

Fiscus, L. & Hyslop, A. (2008). *Career and Technical Student Organizations Reference Guide*, third edition. Available at www.tsaweb.org/sites/default/files/CTSO-Guide.pdf.

Kennedy, B. (1997). *Robert's Rules of Order*—Summary Version. Available at www.robertsrules.org/.

National Coordinating Council for Career and Technical Student Organizations (NCC-CTSO). (2015). Available at www.ctsos.org/.

Threeton, M., Ewing, J. & Clark, R. (2010, Summer). An Informal Analysis of Career and Technical Student Organization Competitive Event Competencies via Kolb's Experiential Learning Theory. *Online Journal of Workforce Education and Development*, (IV)3. Available at http://opensiuc.lib.siu.edu/cgi/viewcontent.cgi?article=1079&context=ojwed.

chapter V
Understanding Student Assessment

Understanding the basics of assessment

Almost everyone is able to ride a bicycle; that's a really good thing from the viewpoint of this author, whose son makes his living in the cycling industry! We suspect that most of you learned to cycle in your early elementary years, or perhaps even younger for you prodigies out there. All of you probably remember some process that involved a number of steps. Chances are, training wheels were involved as well as a supportive friend or relative. As you went through these steps, you experienced a feeling of increasing confidence because you were becoming increasingly more competent. If you experienced some frustration, friends and family helped you to push past it. Those same friends and family members were also watching and *assessing* your current performance to determine if you were competent.

How far can I push you?

Do you remember why you wanted to ride a bicycle in the first place? In many cases it was a combination of factors; maybe you wanted some independence from Mom and Dad, maybe you wanted to go faster than you could run, maybe you wanted to ride a "big kid's" bike, maybe you wanted to ride with your friends or maybe you just wanted to get to a nearby candy store more quickly. Whatever the motivation was for learning to ride your bike, it is clear that you had set this as a goal for yourself. You set a specific goal and you wanted to ensure that you were making progress along the way.

Why assess?

A major reason that assessment is important is because it provides a way to know whether or not you've met your goals. In an educational setting, sometimes those goals are defined by others, like a CTE teacher. As the technical expert, the teacher understands the process that students have to follow toward overall competence. Whether the goal is learning to ride a bike to a local candy store or whether the goal is to become a carpenter, a nurse or a wind turbine technician, there must be a way to measure progress along the way and signal completion of the goal. It's important to understand that this measure needs to be objective and shared with multiple audiences for a variety of reasons.

Who are those multiple audiences if you are a teacher? The audience could be students' parents. As the teacher, you need to be able to tell them how far along their sons or daughters are toward their goal. The audience could be a local administrator or a counselor who has taken an interest in the progress of one of your students. The audience could even be local employers who may be interested in hiring new employees with certain skills and knowledge. Many of these audiences may want to consider more than just the teacher's words, more than just, "Yes, your son is making real progress." They will want to see the evidence or data supporting that "real progress." In some cases an objective third party may be needed to support that evaluation. When CTE teachers have that kind of evidence, they become more credible with all of those audiences.

This section began with the heading 'Why Assess?' and we want to build on that heading a little bit because credibility is critical for new CTE teachers! Having supportive data about the progress of your students is a large part of that credibility. Data result from frequent assessments, but those data have other benefits, too. For example, introspective CTE teachers could evaluate their own instruction by analyzing the test results. They could use the resulting data to form an instructional improvement plan for their class. The information could be used to determine the need for additional equipment, tools or instruments. On the other hand, these assessment data could be used to establish a benchmark for students, an educational plan for moving forward or to justify new equipment. Lastly, the data obtained could be used solely for regulatory purposes. Maybe the local board requires a quarterly general progress report of each of the technical programs; perhaps the state requires an annual report about student competencies or maybe the state is using these data

for a report required by the federal government as a result of something known as the "Perkins Legislation." You'll read more about some assessment basics a little further into this chapter and in the one that follows.

The real bottom line, though, is that assessment has a lot to do with determining quality: program quality, instructional quality and student quality. Think about your definition of quality and how you measure it. This consideration will guide you as you develop and select assessments.

What to assess?

When you were learning to ride that bike, remember the number of steps that you took along the way to become an independent bike rider? Not just riding up and down your driveway, but across your town and in a variety of environments? Did you need just skills, or knowledge AND skills? One of your early steps might have been riding down the driveway with training wheels and ap-

plying the brakes to stop you from going out into the busy street. That activity represented a physical skill, one that required maintaining your balance and applying brakes to preserve your own safety! In addition to the physical parts of your learning, you also had to develop or adapt the knowledge that if you saw a car coming, you had to apply your brakes and stay out of the way. Soon that knowledge transferred to something a little more abstract, an understanding of traffic signs. You recognized that when you saw those red octagons or lights, you had to apply the brakes.

Similarly, it's important that, as the CTE teacher and technical expert, you are able to break up the content of your occupational specialty into learnable pieces. Many times you'll have resources to help you, like state-

or locally implemented programs of study, books, an occupational analysis and the advice of occupational advisory committees, but sometimes your experience in an occupation is the best guide. Whatever resources you use to determine that content, you will also need to determine how best to measure its use. Is it knowledge or is it a skill? How will you make sure that your students understand this? For example, if it is important to use a measuring tool to take a particular measurement, it probably needs to be assessed in multiple ways. You could utilize a worksheet showing linear measurements and ask students to work through that sheet by writing down the measurements and checking them, but is that really the goal? Don't you want them to be able to apply their ability to take a measurement in something closer to a real-life situation?

In some cases, remembering the bicycle training-wheel analogy is helpful. You are building skills from simple to complex, with the final goal being application in a real-life setting. Another factor to consider is the level of acceptance, or what determines a quality score or performance on a given assessment. Referring to the measurement example used earlier, how close to perfect do your students have to get and just what is "perfect" anyway? Are you striving for a general measurement, such as within a foot, or a more precise one, using much smaller divisions, like 1/16th of an inch or one millimeter? As you start to think about building competency, tracking progress and applying skills, you can see that assessment is a big part of the puzzle! Now add in what may be a new term for some of you reading this chapter. The term is *formative*; it's a label given to a type of assessment (Greenstein 2010; Popham 2006). It's the type that CTE teachers design for themselves or it could be those quiz questions at the end of a textbook chapter. The label "formative" means that the assessment is being used to determine progress along the way, a sort of milestone. What follows is a list of some general considerations when designing a formative assessment.

- Determine the goal of the assessment.
- Think deeply about the setting or context where the assessment should take place.
- Decide what type of assessment (paper and pencil, oral, online, performance) should be required.
- Select which tools and resources will be needed for the assessment to be conducted.
- Evaluate whether or not the assessment should be timed (speed test).
- Determine acceptable scores on the assessment.

Cognitive, affective and psychomotor domains

For someone with limited pedagogical skills and/or experience in teaching, the words cognitive, affective and psychomotor can seem like a foreign language. Essentially these words translate to three facets of learning; loosely translated, they represent knowledge-based skills, attitudinal skills and performance skills. Since CTE encompasses all domains of learning, you will need to consider these domains when thinking about assessment. Going back to the analogy of learning to ride a bicycle, a cognitive skill example might be the understanding of how your brakes work. An affective skill example might be showing courtesy to others, such as stopping for someone crossing the street in front of you. Lastly, a psychomotor skill might be using a tool to adjust the brakes. For those of you who want a more formal definition of these domains, it can be found at Miriam Webster's (2015) website www.merriam-webster.com or detailed in Waller (2008) or Anderson and Krathwohl (2001).

Cognitive: relating to, being or involving conscious intellectual activity (thinking, reasoning or remembering)

Affective: relating to, arising from or influencing feelings or emotions

Psychomotor: relating to motor action (physical movement) directly processed from mental activity (brain signal)

For any teacher to have a comprehensive evaluation of a student, more than one type of assessment is necessary (U.S. Department of Labor 2006). The strength of CTE instructional methods is that many, if not all of them, are based on learning to DO something; that means that your focus should be on evaluating how a student performs. That performance is then reinforced by his/her cognitive knowledge and ability to perform it with the expected attitude.

Some CTE educators refer to these three facets as head, heart and hands. If that helps clarify the relationship for you as it relates to testing and assessment, please use it!

One of the ways in which CTE teaching is different is the connection to multiple senses. Research has shown that learning retention is strongly and positively influenced by the number of senses engaged. Edgar Dale's (1969) early work indicated that we remember 10 percent of what we read, 20 percent of what we hear and 30 percent of what we see. When we combine these senses though, we increase the retention rate to more than 50 percent. This engagement of the senses is probably one reason why things learned in a CTE classroom tend to be retained.

"Tell me, I may listen. Teach me, I may remember. Involve me, I will do it." This phrase is attributed to Chinese philosopher Lao Tse, who could have easily been describing CTE. This focus on all senses is a clear benefit of CTE, but it also makes it a bit more difficult to design an appropriate assessment.

Another factor to think about regarding assessment is the level of the type of questions asked. You may have run across Bloom's Taxonomy (Krathwohl 2002) or Webb's Depth of Knowledge (Ferrara, Huff & Lopez 2010) by now; if you have, you'll know that the CTE goal is to get students to the top of the pyramid. That top of the pyramid really translates to students having the ability to apply the skills you've taught them in a variety of settings. In the old version of Bloom, the highest level was "evaluation," meaning a student could evaluate options and select the best course of action. In the newer version of Bloom, the word is "creativity," meaning students can creatively assemble options to solve a given problem. Webb's terminology is "extended thinking," meaning that students make strategic choices about which information they use to solve a given problem. Knowing a little bit about these levels helps you determine what level and what type of assessment you'll be implementing.

Any truly comprehensive evaluation of a student's skills needs to occur multiple times using a variety of assessment tools. These assessment tools should also increase in complexity so that the student has a progressively more challenging opportunity to demonstrate increases in skills and knowledge.

Standardized versus teacher-made assessments

Start with some basic decisions and assume that the goal is to evaluate a student's competency. You are trying to decide whether to use a standardized assessment or a teacher-made assessment. This book is written for CTE teachers who are still within their first year of teaching CTE, so the likelihood is that your exposure to standardized testing has been limited. However, you should know that current federal legislation requires "attainment of career and technical skill proficiencies, including student achievement on technical assessments, that are aligned with industry-recognized standards." Developing these types of assessments cannot be accomplished by an individual and typically come from a third party with the ability to access national data within a given industry. That third-party involvement is part of the definition of a standardized test.

Let's try to explain the two assessment types in a format as basic as possible; first, though, it's important to remember that both of these assessments were based on some form of standards. The current focus in CTE is on the implementation of a POS (National Association of State Directors of Career Technical Education Consortium, 2011). This POS is based on a course sequence and curriculum that reflects accepted industry standards. Though industry standards may look very different based upon the field that they represent, they typically refer to major components of industry processes, procedures, equipment, tools, instruments, safety, technical manuals/blueprints, etc. When a student has completed the secondary portion of the POS, they are usually considered CTE "completers." Most often a third-party standardized test is used that reflects comprehensive knowledge and skills in a particular industry.

In the bicycle analogy, the accepted standards for bicycle riding could be: pedaling, turning, braking, rules of the road and maintenance. Most assume that these are agreed-upon national standards and that you, as the parent, have deemed that your son or daughter is competent at bicycling. You probably have based that assumption of competence on watching your "pupil" demonstrate his or her knowledge of peddling, turning, braking, as well as knowledge of the rules of the road and bicycle care. Perhaps you made an assessment in each area of this performance. In this example you, the parent, serve as the teacher and you have made an evaluation of the competence of your pupil in each of the standard areas. Perhaps for rules of the road you quizzed your pupil on what to do in certain scenarios. You may have made some sort of performance evaluation of your pupil's ability to pedal smoothly while maintaining proper balance.

Okay, so maybe you weren't this analytical when teaching your son or daughter to ride a bicycle, but you made some sort of assessment or evaluation to allow you to feel comfortable with your child's new independence. This is similar to what you will do as a CTE teacher. You establish an assessment of some small component of your technical area, perhaps the ability to complete an estimate of materials to fabricate a product or the ability to make a patient comfortable while preparing him/her for a medical procedure. You design that assessment based on content you have taught that is linked to some component of a nationally accepted standard.

Now think specifically about a standardized test. Using the bicycle example, the fact that you, as the teacher, have conducted the instruction and deemed that your pupil is a competent rider may not be good enough. Maybe you were too strict or maybe you were a little too lenient; it is your child after all! What if someone else with subject matter expertise were asked to evaluate your child's riding ability?

What if the local bicycle shops were willing to have staff evaluate your child's riding ability based on *standards* established by the League of American Bicyclists? They evaluate based on the same recognized standards that you taught your child (pedaling, turning, braking, etc.), but they do it on a Saturday afternoon with a standardized bicycle navigation course and perhaps a written test asking your child to respond to different scenarios encompassing all areas of riding a bicycle.

A standardized test is usually what educators refer to as a *summative* test—one that is given to measure learning at the conclusion of a program of study or an entire course; in other words, a final exam. In simplistic terms, the similarities between a standardized test and a teacher-constructed test can be described this way: both tests have two steps in common. Both types of tests involve planning the test (selecting the standards on which it will be based) and also preparing the test items that measure the standards (Educational Testing Service, 2015). Guidelines should be used to make sure that the test items are well-constructed and reflect the standards or content that is being taught (Nebraska Dept. of Education, 2015). The difference with a standardized test is that it includes two additional steps. One step involves an experimental administration, or piloting, of the test before it is finalized. The other step with a standardized assessment is a formal process for controlling the environment in which the test is administered. Most educational testing specialists will tell you that there are many more differences involved, such as the experiences of the people who were involved in designing the test questions and the manuals that describe the statistics involved that made the test credible, but for now this description of a standardized test should be sufficient.

As a new CTE teacher, you should know that both standardized and teacher-made tests are part of your new toolkit. They provide an opportunity to watch your students grow and become increasingly competent in their respective fields.

How to select a standardized assessment

You should become familiar with nationally validated CTE assessments because every time you have a group of program completers, chances are that they will be taking a standardized assessment of some sort. Helping each group of students continually improve their technical competence not only makes you and your school look good, it also helps to ensure that your state continues to receive federal funding supporting CTE programming.

Many states have a list of approved standardized technical assessments that can be administered to program completers. In some cases, teachers themselves have little flexibility in selecting an end-of-program assessment. However, if your state allows you to select from a list of options, or if you are fortunate enough to be able to make the selection on your own with the approval of your local administrator, then here are some questions you should answer as you make that selection:

1. Is there an alignment between the assessment standards and the questions when compared to the technical components of your program of study?
2. In addition to a total score, do the reports from the standardized assessment provide detailed information (more than a pass/fail designation) that can be used as the basis for instructional improvement?
3. Are there accommodations for students with individualized educational plans (IEPs)?
4. Is personalized customer service readily available before, during and after test administration?
5. Are tools available to help you prepare your students for the test (pretests, study guides or practice questions)?
6. Is the organization that developed the assessment reputable and recognized within the CTE community?
7. Is the assessment development process based on industry testing standards (American Psychological Association, American Educational Testing Research Association, etc.)?
8. Are additional costs associated with using the standardized assessment? For example, does the school itself or the program need to be certified or accredited? Is a subscription cost involved? Are there membership fees?

In most cases these issues will be handled by your school's administration, but chances are good that, over the course of your career, you will be involved in selecting an assessment for an educational purpose. Keep these minimum criteria handy. You never know when you might be asked for input.

Tools for your toolbox

This chapter talks about teacher-made tests vs. third-party tests, and it was mentioned that one of the first steps regarding assessment was determining why you are doing any kind of assessment. The following example from a third-year Baking & Pastry Arts Program teacher indicates that the goals were relationship-building and benchmarking. This teacher needed to get to know her "new class" during that first year and she needed to do it quickly!

I was told that several of my seniors had a fairly high competence level, so to verify this, I created a quick written assessment asking basic-to-advanced questions about baking, and I added in some baking math basics. The results were not what I expected. I passed along the results to the administrator and knew that I would have to start from the ground up on the theory and knowledge content lessons. I also created a kitchen assessment to see how students worked in the kitchen. I checked for organization, cleanliness, their ingredient knowledge and most importantly their measuring and recipe reading abilities. These two assessments gave me an idea of where to start with the students. I was happy to be on ground zero; although many of the students did not agree with me, the test results supported my position.

Here is a list of potential areas that can be explored with a teacher-made test.

- Determine your students' shop/lab/clinic hands-on abilities.
- Determine their baseline knowledge in your content area.
- Determine their scope and exposure to math-related concepts.
- Determine their individual resilience (How do they react to testing and testing results?).
- Determine their integrity, personality types and maturity levels.
- Determine their learning styles.
- Figure out what motivates them (good grades, rewards, fear of failure, social aspects and natural curiosity).
- Determine their writing ability/knowledge.
- Determine their reading and comprehension ability.
- Identify what part parents/guardians play in the students' education (supportive/available/works all the time/stay at home/etc.).
- Figure out what other interests students have outside the classroom (music, art, dance, video games, sports, etc.).

This example is from the reflections of a child care teacher and focuses on assuring that teacher-developed tests require students to do more than just remember factoids.

When I first began teaching my Early Childhood Care and Education program, I naturally relied on the unit tests provided by the publisher of the text. I can remember emphasizing the facts, but facts that stood alone and facts that only required recall in order to answer the multiple choice question at hand. I wondered what they retained? After reflecting on my assessment choices, I remembered that CTE teaching is about "doing" and applying, not about memorizing. I began to set up my assessments taking Bloom's Taxonomy into account; if they were to be successful they needed to do more than just remembering, memorizing and recalling. I wanted my students creating, synthesizing, evaluating and designing. I began to create my assessments around enhanced learning projects, high- interest activities and tiered assignments that incorporated things like flexible grouping. In my current teaching, I often review a matrix of words associated with each of the conceptual thinking levels and I cross-check that with my assessments to assure the inclusion of concepts requiring higher-order thinking skills.

In addition to looking at the depth of the questions, sometimes it's good to use another set of eyes. Here's a reflection from a welding teacher.

I remember as a new welding instructor that I was developing a test for one of the courses that I taught and I was having my wife proofread it. After she was done proofing it, I asked her to actually see how she would score on it (it was some multiple choice, fill in the blank and matching). Let me remind you that my wife did not know anything about welding (except that it made sparks and smoke). Needless to say, she passed the test with a 70 percent, if I remember correctly! I was blown away that she could pass a test and yet knew very little about the content. I went back through each item and she told me how she arrived at the answer. I was truly amazed that someone could pass a test in an area they had no knowledge about with just some basic common sense and general test-taking skills.

Since we mentioned the affective domain, we thought we'd share an example of a tool that emphasizes positive work ethic brought to us by some teachers in Kansas.

Through the help of my colleague, we have developed a unique way of managing our labs and classrooms through the use of a "token" system. This system is used to help evaluate a student's workplace readiness skills. This evaluation has been subjective in the past and we were looking for a more objective approach to evaluating student ethics.

At the beginning of the semester, the students are given four "tokens." Students are told that these tokens are worth a combined total of 100 points. During the semester if a student commits an ethical violation (defined at the start of the semester) or is found using unsafe practices in the lab, the student can have a token taken from them. Students can also earn tokens back by going above and beyond what is expected (also defined at the start of the year). The "tokens" are also used to borrow tools from the shop's tool room, so maintaining all 4 tokens allows the student to borrow four individual tools to work on various projects.

Though the next chapter addresses some of the specifics of performance test development, we thought it important to include some experiences regarding the design of complex-skill application test from an auto mechanics teacher. Sometimes these sorts of evaluations show that there may be a number of correct methods to solve a problem in addition to the one the teacher presented.

I sat down to devise a comprehensive four-wheel alignment test. The questions I wanted answered were: Does the student know what the alignment angles are? How do they relate to each other? How do they affect the steering characteristics of the vehicle and what will the tire wear be? The test I came up with gave the student a vehicle year, make and model.

Students had to use a service manual to find and document alignment specifications. Then they had to retrieve the alignment angles I had recorded on the alignment machine. I call this the 'data retrieval' part of the test. The student then had to compare two sets of angles and answer several questions. This part required the student to compare and analyze (higher-level Bloom). The readings on the alignment machine were all within specification except the toe. (Toe refers to the alignment of a wheel compared to the centerline of a vehicle.) In question one, the student had to decide if the car would drive correctly and if not they had to describe what would happen? In the second question the student had to determine if and what type of tire wear the present alignment will cause? With the last question they had to decide what alignment angles need adjustment and in what order?

I set the alignment angles so that they were at the edge of their specification in such a way that any one angle would not cause a problem, but two or more added together could lead to steering concerns. The three questions were answered using the student's knowledge and problem solving skills and shared with the class as a whole. This format provided the students an opportunity to analyze the problem and hear different perspectives from their peers. The conversations that followed provided not only whether the students understood the concepts, but also revealed different and correct ways to solve a technical problem.

This overview provided some basics regarding assessment and testing and focused on discussing student evaluation, but that's only half of the power of assessment. The next chapter will explain that the real power of assessment lies in its ability to continuously improve the quality of instruction, and some more will be shared about testing student competence as well.

KEY LEARNINGS:

1. Tests are used as a tool to evaluate student competence.
2. Assessment is important to assure quality.
3. Comprehensive student evaluation involves assessing multiple aspects of a student's knowledge and skills.
4. Formative tests are generally teacher-made and show progress toward a goal.
5. Standardized summative assessments frequently utilize a pretesting option.
6. An important consideration for standardized test selection is alignment to industry standards.

RELATED CONTENT THAT MAY BE OF INTEREST:

Anderson, L.W. (Ed.), Krathwohl, D.R. (Ed.), Airasian, P.W., Cruikshank, K.A., Mayer, R.E., Pintrich, P.R., Raths, J., & Wittrock, M.C. (2001). *A Taxonomy for Learning, Teaching and Assessing: A Revision of Bloom's Taxonomy of Educational Objectives* (Complete edition). New York: Longman.

Carl D Perkins Career and Technical Education Act of 2006.

Dale, E. (1969). *Audiovisual Methods in Teaching*. NY: Dryden Press. Retrieved June 11, 2015, www.etsu.edu/uged/etsu1000/documents/Dales_Cone_of_Experience.pdf.

Educational Testing Service. (2015). How Tests and Test Questions are Developed. Princeton, NJ: author. Retrieved June 11, 2015 www.ets.org/understanding_testing/test_development/.

Ferrara, S., Huff, K. & Lopez, E. (2010). Targeting Cognition in Item Design to Enhance Valid Interpretations of Test Performances: A Case Study and Some Speculations. A paper presented in S. Ferrara & K. Huff (Chairs), *Cognition and Valid Inferences About Student Achievement: Aligning Items with Cognitive and Proficiency Targets*. Denver, CO: Cognition and Assessment Special Interest Group symposium conducted at the annual meeting of the American Educational Research Association.

RELATED CONTENT THAT MAY BE OF INTEREST, continued:

Greenstein, L. (2010). *What Teachers Really Need to Know About Formative Assessment.* Alexandria, VA: ASCD. Retrieved June 11, 2015 www.ascd.org/publications/books/110017/chapters/The-Fundamentals-of-Formative-Assessment.aspx.

Krathwohl, D. R. (2002). A Revision of Bloom's Taxonomy: *An overview. Theory Into Practice,* 41(4), Autumn 2002. 212-218. Retrieved June 11, 2015 www.unco.edu/cetl/sir/stating_outcome/documents/Krathwohl.pdf.

Merriam-Webster (2015). Merriam-Webster's Collegiate Dictionary. Springfield, MA: Merriam-Webster, Incorporated.

Murray, J. (1905). *The Sayings of Lao-Tzu.* London, England: Hazell Watson and Viney Ltd.

National Association of State Directors of Career Technical Education Consortium. (2011). *Building Comprehensive Programs of Study Through Progressive State Career and Technical Legislation.* Silver Spring, MD: National Association of State Directors of Career Technical Education. Retrieved June 11, 2015, www.careertech.org/sites/default/files/Principle4-CTE-POS-2011.pdf.

Nebraska Department of Education. (2015). *Item Writing Guidelines.* Lincoln NE: author. Retrieved June 11, 2015, www.education.ne.gov/Assessment/pdfs/C4L/Item_Writing_Guidelines.pdf.

Popham, W. J. (2006). *Defining and Enhancing Formative Assessment.* Paper presented at the Annual Large-Scale Assessment Conference, Council of Chief State School Officers, San Francisco, CA.

U.S. Department of Labor, Employment and Training Administration. (2006). *Testing and Assessment: A Guide to Good Practices for Workforce Investment Professionals.*

Waller, K. V. (2008). *Writing Instructional Objectives.* Rosemont, IL: National Accrediting Agency for Clinical Laboratory Sciences. Retrieved June 11, 2015, www.naacls.org/docs/announcement/writing-objectives.pdf.

Washington, DC, U.S. Department of Labor. Retrieved June 11, 2015, www.onetcenter.org/dl_files/proTestAsse.pdf.

chapter VI
Assessment Data and Instructional Improvement

Can you
evaluate you?

Can you evaluate yourself?

Teaching is a "contract" between teacher and learner, and communication really has to be a two-way street. If a student doesn't want to learn, then both the contract and the relationship are null and void. By the same token, if the teacher isn't willing to consider ways to improve his or her craft, the same contract/relationship is null and void. The communication has to be open and honest enough to be free from a student's and/or a teacher's ego. This unofficial contract is even more critical in a CTE environment because of the additional amount of time the student spends with the teacher—the adult mentor. Mentors must deliver honest and objective feedback about a student's progress throughout his or her learning, but also "take stock" of their own abilities and be willing to improve their skills as CTE teachers. This willingness to change and improve can enhance the teacher-student relationship. Assessment is often consic a means to evaluate a student's level of proficiency and it is that; it is also a self-evaluation tool for the teacher. It is the objective analysis of student test data that can provide the basis for instructional improvement.

We spent some time in the last chapter talking about the bicycle analogy and about someone administering a standardized assessment for your child's bicycling skills. But what we didn't talk about was how a standardized test and the formative criteria used to check his or her abilities along the way impacts your training of the next child. Did you, as the bicycling teacher, learn about your instruction from your first child's instruction? What things would you have done differently, and how might you be able to improve your instruction for this next child?

Pretests, formative tests and summative tests

The difference between formative and summative tests was discussed in the last chapter. The focus of the previous chapter, though, was on finding out if a student was making progress. The goal in the bicycling analogy was to help the new cyclist achieve competence. What if we looked at it through a different lens? What if, as you were teaching your bicycling trainee, you took time to reflect upon how you yourself could improve your bicycle training skills. Maybe if several measures of how far back from the stop sign your trainee stopped were available, this would've constituted some measurable outcome data. Assessments in CTE are a way to see not only how students are doing, but also how the teacher is doing. By using "student outcome data" from objective assessments, what information can be gathered about the instruction? Is the instructor helping the group make progress towards competency? Is the instructor able to adjust instruction to continually improve it? Every child learns differently, and it is important that teachers try to customize their instruction for those individual abilities as best they can. One way to gauge whether or not instruction is effective is by using the tools of student assessment and evaluation as a means to improve instruction.

In most CTE programs, students spend more than the traditional 120 clock hours with the teacher. Program lengths vary by class time, number of periods in a day and number of years in a program. However, regardless of the time involved, certain things are common; one should always establish some sort of "baseline" level of skills and knowledge for the student and the overall class. This "baseline" usually consists of an assessment of background knowledge prior to receiving instruction (NOCTI, 2015; Institute of Education Sciences, 2015). This assessment is generally more objective if it is from a third-party source and the content of the assessment has been predetermined to be in alignment with your local POS. As the student begins his or her instruction in the technical specialty, a baseline test of some sort should be administered. This test covers the major areas of content within the technical area and helps illuminate in which areas of content the students have little background. From an overall classroom perspective, this information helps provide the teacher with a broad picture of which areas may require more instructional time.

As an example, perhaps a baseline measure or pretest indicated that your students had a fairly good understanding of body systems (circulatory, respiratory, digestive etc.), but as a class they had a lot of difficulty with medical terminology. As you look at your long-range planning (how much time you anticipate spending on certain areas of instruction), you might conclude that you could spend less time on body systems and more time on terminology. Maybe other hints from the pretest indicate that you should redesign your instructional methods a little bit—maybe spend some time with Latin root-words to assist with the medical terminology. The point is that you will be able to adjust your classroom instruction based on real-time objective data.

On the individual level, let's say that during that same pretest you had one student who scored extremely poorly in body systems, unlike the

majority of the class. Rather than holding up an entire class until that student catches up, you decide to work with that individual student to get him/her up-to-speed with the rest of the class. Again, this requires the teacher to be willing to make instructional adaptations based on the results of the pretest so that all students can be successful. In most cases it is best if this pretest or baseline test is from a third party and that the pretest is closely tied to the post-test or summative test, which would occur at the end of the instructional program. This pretest would be based on an objective set of industry standards which would assure that the test content is relevant and that any subjectivity in scoring is eliminated. From a teacher planning perspective, pretesting really helps to identify instructional targets and goals for the teacher, in addition to those of the students.

A formative test is one that could come at the end of a unit and is designed by the teacher for student evaluation, usually of a major piece of content (Ferlazzo, 2014; Hattie, 2003). Yes, a formative test is an indication of whether or not the teacher conveyed the information about medical terminology to the students, but it also gives the teacher an indicator of whether or not there is a need to review portions of this unit again or perhaps reinforce the students' content knowledge by using a different instructional technique. Perhaps during the formative assessment on medical terminology the students did quite well with suffixes, prefixes and root words. They even did well with medical definitions and accepted abbreviations, but for some reason they had difficulty with "body planes" (body planes refers to universal directional terminology when identifying locations on a body.) Depending on the number of students having difficulty with the concept, the teacher may choose to re-teach the concept immediately or might just choose to include some emphasis on directional terms in the upcoming units. The teacher may even consider utilizing a verbal quiz to do a bit of checking for understanding on a regular basis. As you become more experienced as a teacher, you will develop more options for delivering content. The purpose of this chapter is to raise awareness of the dual diagnostic power of assessment; as a CTE professional, your powers of analysis will continue to develop over time.

A summative assessment, in CTE, has come to mean a test given at the conclusion of a program, it is an assessment that would be given to program completers in CTE. An end-of-program summative assessment is typically best accomplished through a third party. That assessment is based on standards that are nationally accepted and linked to a POS. The summative assessment brings objectivity, reliability and validation into the mix (Glazer, 2014). Objectivity, in this context, means that the test was designed by a group and included members who were disconnected from the instruction of the students taking the test, but not from the standards on which the instruction was based. That may sound a bit strange, but the idea is that the teacher delivering instruction to a group has a relationship with that group and it is difficult to be objective, even with effort.

Objectivity is also important when looking at the big picture. A person who loves teaching a particular area of content may spend weeks on it, hoping that the students will also come to enjoy it. The reality may be, though, that from a national perspective, that area of content is relatively unimportant in developing a technician with overall competence. Reliability, in terms of a summative assessment, means that the test has a track record of consistency and has been used with audiences made up of the same kinds of students who are in your class. It means that the test is credible. The term validity means that this test has been checked against standards deemed appropriate by SMEs who understand industry standards (Educational Testing Service, 2015).

The bottom line is that in addition to evaluating the individual, student outcome data from pretests, formative and summative tests can be used just as effectively by the teacher to plan and adjust instruction as they can be to evaluate a student's current competency level. To put it in its simplest context, a pretest can be used by the teacher to help estimate the amount of time over a given course that the teacher should plan to spend on each different piece of content. It can also help the teacher figure out which students may need individual coaching or assistance. The formative teacher-developed test provides information that teachers can use to modify or adjust instruction along the way (Ferlazzo, 2014; Hattie, 2003). Lastly, the summative test can provide the teachers with information on how successful they have been with different cohorts of students (Institute of Education Science, 2015). Once teachers have a few years under their belt, it is interesting to see if their instructional techniques are improving or staying static, regardless of the class composition. Did the 2015 class of completers have a better understanding of anatomical planes than the 2014 class? Students' advancement can be proven using tests as a measure of technique and not just their retention of information.

Benchmarking and pretesting

Typically teachers, regardless of their area of content expertise, recognize that there are a variety of roles for assessment throughout the teaching and learning process (Cromey, 2000; Foster, Hodes & Pritz, 2014). Without walking through all of these roles, it is important to list some of them:

- Assessments can help clarify the goals of the learning for the student.
- Assessments can help the teacher better understand the existing competency level of the CTE student.
- Assessments can serve to motivate CTE students.
- Assessments can increase retention and transfer of learning for CTE students.
- Assessments can help with diagnosing and remediating shortcomings in a CTE student's skills or knowledge.
- Assessments can guide student grouping for instruction or possibly peer teaching.
- Assessments can help determine if re-teaching concepts is necessary.

Several of these roles can be addressed to some degree by one specific type of test, usually known as a pretest, mentioned earlier in this chapter. A pretest can help the teacher establish a baseline of knowledge and skill in content areas. A pretest not only helps the teacher understand the existing competencies a particular student may possess, but also may be a guide to diagnosing where overall classroom deficits exist. A pretest, then, could serve as both a diagnostic tool for the individual student and for the class as a whole; in turn, this helps the teacher focus on specific areas of instruction.

Although pretests can be developed by teachers themselves or by a third party (Educational Testing Service 2015), it is best to make these assessments as objective as possible. Just as important as the objectivity is the alignment to a set of national standards and a national perspective for which some competencies are more critical than others. This kind of assessment requires input from a variety of current SMEs and related industry associations across the country. These kinds of resources are typically difficult for a local teacher to gather. An added benefit to utilizing a third-party pretest is that the same organization delivering pretests typically has summative post-tests available as well. This is the case with NOCTI technical assessments; more information about pretests can be found online in the "Assessments" section at www.nocti.org/Pre-Testing.cfm?m=2. The other advantage of standardized third-party testing is the fact that the score reports are also standardized; those reports help the teacher to get a more objective view of the industry-related skills and knowledge their students should know at the conclusion of the program.

Let's take a look at the kinds of information that can be gleaned from a third-party pretest. The test report below is from the written portion of a Welding Pretest (NOCTI, 2015).

Std #	Description of the Standard Area	Student A	Student B	Student C	Student D	Student E	Class Average
1	Safety	72.7	69.2	42.7	70.1	67.4	64.4
2	Welding Symbols and Blueprint Reading	90.9	83.2	54.9	71.2	75.9	75.2
3	Oxyfuel Cutting (OFC)	52.6	63.7	49.2	64.0	56.3	57.2
4	Arc Cutting Process (Carbon Arc and Plasma Arc)	47.6	58.4	56.1	56.7	67.3	57.2
5	Physical Characteristics and Mechanical Properties of Metals	71.4	68.5	47.6	73.4	76.8	67.5
6	Weld Fit-Up and Quality	57.1	75.7	59.8	62.3	69.0	64.8
7	Shielded Metal Arc Welding (SMAW)	64.7	74.1	49.3	63.7	69.1	64.2
8	Gas Metal Arc Welding (GMAW) and Flux Cored Arc Welding (FCAW)	47.1	62.4	32.1	44.2	46.3	46.4
9	Gas Tungsten Arc Welding (GTAW)	45.3	65.0	29.8	43.3	48.0	46.3
	TOTAL	61.0	68.9	46.8	61.0	64.0	60.4

Upon initial inspection by the teacher, the table reveals some important information about the class. It shows that in the area of "Welding Symbols and Blueprint Reading" the class has an unusually high pretest score. This means that there is existing knowledge on which the teacher may be able to capitalize. It also shows that the one student, "Student C", who did not do as well as the others did not do well on any of the major areas and would probably benefit from some one-on-one coaching.

Std #	Description of the Standard Area	Student A	Student B	Student C	Student D	Student E	Class Average
1	Safety	72.7	69.2	42.7	70.1	67.4	64.4
2	Welding Symbols and Blueprint Reading	90.9	83.2	54.9	71.2	75.9	75.2
3	Oxyfuel Cutting (OFC)	52.6	63.7	49.2	64.0	56.3	57.2
4	Arc Cutting Process (Carbon Arc and Plasma Arc)	47.6	58.4	56.1	56.7	67.3	57.2
5	Physical Characteristics and Mechanical Properties of Metals	71.4	68.5	47.6	73.4	76.8	67.5
6	Weld Fit-Up and Quality	57.1	75.7	59.8	62.3	69.0	64.8
7	Shielded Metal Arc Welding (SMAW)	64.7	74.1	49.3	63.7	69.1	64.2
8	Gas Metal Arc Welding (GMAW) and Flux Cored Arc Welding (FCAW)	47.1	62.4	32.1	44.2	46.3	46.4
9	Gas Tungsten Arc Welding (GTAW)	45.3	65.0	29.8	43.3	48.0	46.3
	TOTAL	61.0	68.9	46.8	61.0	64.0	60.4

Delving further using the chart one can begin to see some other information about individuals within the class. "Student A," for example, may be able to help others with the area of "Welding Symbols and Blueprint Reading." There may be an opportunity to pair "Student A" with "Student C" for this unit. Notice that although "Student A" has a high score in one area of content, "Student B" has the highest overall scores in most of the areas. Lastly, it would be important to note that the last two major areas of content involving gas welding are "low scoring" across all members of the class. This is likely an area to which the teacher will have to dedicate more instructional time.

Unit tests and quizzes

In earlier paragraphs, information was presented that could be obtained by the teacher based on scores from a pretest. Once the year has begun and instruction has started, the next level of testing that a typical CTE teacher might use are quizzes and unit tests.

A few pages ago, a mock report showed major standards in the area of welding. These major areas are the focus of a student's technical competence that should be achieved by the conclusion of the technical training. Here is a list of major areas in Carpentry (NOCTI 2015):

1. Safety
2. Tools and Accessories
3. Blueprint Reading and Estimation Skills
4. Foundation, Forms and Concrete
5. Rough Framing
6. Exterior Finish
7. Interior Systems Installation
8. Interior Finish
9. Carpentry-related Mathematics

Note that these major units of information are typically related to a piece of equipment, a procedure, a tool or a service performed. In carpentry, for example, many of the major areas are tied to a phase of the construction of a structure (foundation, rough framing, exterior trim, interior trim, etc.). In precision machining they may be tied to a piece of equipment (lathe, mill, grinder, CNC machine, etc.). The point is that the instructor may need considerable teaching time until a student acquires all the knowledge and skills within these major units. These major units typically require some sort of formative unit test. This testing is considered formative because the teacher will still be able to use the results of this test to adjust the instruction with the present group of students.

Think about the example of rough framing in the construction trade. Subunits within that larger unit deal with individual components that make up the skeleton of the building, like walls, floors, roofs and stairs. A unit exam on rough framing would be a rather large unit test. In order to assure student comprehension, it needs to be broken into even smaller units. This is where field experience will help. Assuming there is a decision to break the units into unit tests on each area of framing, it is necessary to determine what the purpose of that test is. Chances are it is to assess student knowledge, but a test like that tells as much about instruction as it does about students' learning.

What does this mean? Well, if 90 percent of the students missed a question on part of this test, what happened? Was the question misworded? Was the question one of a group of questions on a particular concept and other questions on that concept were missed too? Generally if more than 35 percent of the students miss something on a unit test, chances are good that it was an instructional issue and not a student issue. By the way, a more formal term for analyzing a question is "item analysis." It's about looking question by question at the results of any test to figure out what happened in the instruction.

Another assessment tool teachers have at their disposal is the quiz— a short assessment on smaller amounts of information. Quizzes can be used to keep the class engaged, to check for understanding, to reinforce information or to motivate. Quizzes can be verbal, written or electronically assisted. They can be class-focused or individually focused. This does not cover all the types of tests at a teacher's disposal, but gives some sense of how they can be used as tools to improve instruction.

To give an example of the use of a quiz from the health care field, consider a unit that deals with body systems. This unit includes the respiratory system, which helps people breathe, and the circulatory system, which gets blood and oxygen to the organs. After spending some time giving her students a basic review of the systems' functions, Mrs. Smith decides to give her students a quiz on a sheet of paper at the end of the week. The paper contains two columns of words. One column lists the eleven systems of the body, and on the other column is a two- or three-word description of the system's function. The student is asked to connect the systems with the short definitions. The quiz usually involves small amounts of information, which makes it easy for the instructor to verify the instruction that has been provided. Quizzes are typically informal, impromptu and test current knowledge. In other words, there is typically no time for the student to prepare.

A lot of ground has been covered in this section to point out the connection between using industry-driven standards and formative major unit tests to assess both teaching and learning.

Performance projects

Many CTE students are able to connect the dots from theory to practice in the lab, clinic or shop floor. It is important to create opportunities for students to test their ability to apply these skills in as close to a "real-world" environment as can be provided for them. CTE students could be given a wide variety of performance projects and an equally large number of ways are possible to evaluate that performance. The performance could entail transferring a patient from a gurney to a bed; it could be laying out a common roof rafter or it might be making something by following a recipe or a blueprint. The evaluations could be focused on safe operation of tools and equipment, completion of the work according to standards of quality, or completing the activity in a specified period of time. The scale of the evaluation could be pass/fail or a scale indicating proficiency ranging from 1 to 10.

Performance tests can take a long period of time or a short period of time. They can focus on evaluating a process (the way a student goes about doing something), the product (the adequacy of what the student has built), or both. The important thing about these performance projects is that they show which students are growing in their skills and competence. These projects give the CTE teacher a perfect opportunity for one-on-one coaching and also provide the teacher with clues about how to best teach a particular group. In a large unit test it is important for the CTE teacher to give the students notice that they will be performing a task, tell them about the conditions under which it will be performed, what materials and resources they can use and what standards will be used in the evaluation of the project.

Grading

The concept of grading is one that is generally difficult for teachers to deal with, because it involves not only numbers and letters that signify a student's competence on a given subject, but also a personal philosophy and a bit of human psychology. Here are some underlying questions teachers ask themselves: Do I want my students to respect me because

I am the keeper of all technical knowledge? Do I believe that no one is perfect so no one deserves an "A" or a 100 percent proficiency? Do I want to appear tough or do I want to appear lenient? These are just a few of the many factors in determining someone's score and assigning it a grade that is "universally understood" by others. The best advice on grading is simple: be objective and be consistent.

So what is a grade, really? Simply put, a grade is a categorization of a group or range of scores. Generally, that grouping is reflected in a letter. For example an "A" might mean a score between 100 percent and 90 percent, a "B" might be for the range of 89 percent to 80 percent, etc. A variety of ranges can be used here, but the important thing to remember is that most schools and colleges will require some sort of grade for the students in their program. That grade may also be viewed by others, such as parents, teachers, potential employers and other educational administrators. Chances are good that each one of those groups will have a different interpretation of what the grade actually says about the student who earned it and the teacher that assigned it. Of course, CTE professionals can't control perceptions, so again the advice is to be objective and consistent.

You should be able to convert each student's score on a given test or quiz to a grade on a grading scale. This is a two-step process. The first part is mathematical. Consider the example of a formative medical-abbreviations test that consists of 34 questions. "Student A" gets 33 out of 34 correct, "Student B" gets 31 out of 34 and "Student C" gets 28 out of 34. The most common way to determine a percentage on a test is to take the total number of correct answers and divide it by the total number of questions. In the example of Students A, B and C, Student A's percentage score would be 97 percent (33/34), Student B's percentage would be 91 percent (31/34) and Student C's percentage would be 82 percent (28/34). The next phase of determining a grade involves identifying which range of scores that percentage fits into. For the scale in which an "A" represents percentages falling between 100-90, Students A and B both fall into the "A" range, but for a scale that indicates an "A" is for those scoring at 100-95, this would mean that Student A still receives an "A" but Student B receives something less, probably a "B."

You can see that this is where the subjectivity of grading starts to appear. Although most people have the perception that an "A" signifies a score of relative excellence, suppose that someone used a scale that was outside the norm, perhaps designating 100-80 for an "A." For someone who did not see the scale used, it would be difficult to know the difference between someone scoring at a 99 percent compared to someone scoring at an 81 percent, because both of them received the same grade of "A." Again consistency and honesty are recommended when determining grades. Luckily, most school systems publish and provide teachers with the accepted range of percentages for letter grades.

For the student, a grade can be a motivator or something that demotivates. It can be an evaluation of progress from semester to semester. For an engaged parent, it will almost certainly be used to evaluate the student's progress. For example, a parent might say, "Last semester you received an 'A' in health assisting. What happened that dropped this semester's grade to a 'C'?" Subjectivity may enter in because grading really is about placing a score in a range of scores; since that grade is being determined by a human being—the teacher— some subjectivity can enter in.

The reality is that a good CTE teacher will rely on competency tracking, daily effort, as well as assessment to really know where the student's competency stands. This should not be construed to mean that grading is unimportant, just that it may not be the most precise indicator of a student's progress. For the purposes of this chapter on using data for instructional improvement, it should be noted that assignment of a grade can be subjective and probably shouldn't be used as part of the data to form the basis of instructional improvement decisions. Instructional quality may be generally inferred by the number of a certain letter grade given to a student, like the number of "As" or "Fs," but for the most part it is difficult to use grades as a tool for improving instruction.

Item analysis

It has been said that a teaching flaw equals a learning flaw. Though this is probably an oversimplification, it is certainly something every CTE teacher needs to think about. Unlike most other education disciplines, CTE teachers are hired based on their experience, as opposed to a documentation of their knowledge about a subject. In addition, a CTE teacher hired in a particular discipline is usually the only SME in that building. The ability to apply practical knowledge to make improvement in a product or a process is key for this teacher.

That ability to look at key factors, make a decision and apply solutions isn't just the domain of the technicians being trained in CTE classrooms and labs. Analyzing student output data, making decisions about instructional solutions based on that data and adjusting instruction accordingly is the domain of the CTE teacher as well. This change in instruction increases the skills and competence of that teacher's class and it enhances individual teaching ability as well. One way that teachers can see how they are doing is by using something called a test item analysis (Boudett, Murnane, City & Moody, 2005). Not a formal item analysis involving statistical processes like discrimination indices, standard deviation or standard error of measurement, but more of an informal overview of test data on major CTE content reflecting how teachers can improve their instruction.

The content of a teacher-developed test, or any test for that matter, shouldn't be a secret as the content of the test needs to be aligned to the content of the curriculum, which should be communicated loud and clear to students. Ideally, students should see tests as fair measures of their skills and competencies and a way of underscoring the student-teacher relationship that quality CTE teachers develop.

Performing an item analysis is pretty straightforward, but it does require a commitment of time and a repression of one's ego. After student testing has been completed and you have reviewed the test and determined which questions were incorrect on each student's paper, make a list of all of the questions on a test. Let's say there were 35 of them and 20 students took the test. Make a list of the number of students who missed each question, maybe even put the initials of the student who missed the question on that list. Once the tallies are made, take a critical look at any question that a significant number of students (say, five or more) got wrong. As you look at each of these items, think about quality. Was the question ambiguously worded? Did you use terms your students hadn't heard yet? Did the question have an error (maybe a small math error)? If the majority of the class got a question wrong and you determine that it was a poor question, it makes sense to eliminate it all together. Make the total 34 instead of 35. Once any "bad questions" have been accounted for, it's time to look at what the results say about your teaching. Repeating what was said earlier, if 35 percent of the students got a question wrong and the question based on the concept was error free, it isn't a learning problem—it's a teaching problem.

"I taught it; they just didn't get it," is a common reaction when looking at this kind of data. That's why it's important to keep one's ego out of the analysis. Yes, students do have a responsibility to learn content, but a good teacher will follow up and adjust lesson plans so that he or she can assure student success. Without taking time to build a strong foundation, student understanding of future concepts that build on this foundation may be affected. Successful coaches do something similar. They not only evaluate game day performance, they evaluate practices too, and they take the time to build in individual corrections if the fundamentals seem a bit out of alignment.

Here's a short illustration from a protective services test. Generally, protective services programs cover content in three general areas: law enforcement, fire protection and emergency medical procedures. Mr. Neuteach finished teaching a unit on general public safety; included in that unit was content addressing sanitation procedures, key regulatory agencies, first responder rules and liability issues. The results from Mr. Neuteach's analysis revealed that three-quarters of the class answered questions related to sanitation issues incorrectly. This foundational topic affects all of the protective service specialties and is certainly critical to an Emergency Medical

Technician (EMT.) Mr. Neuteach wisely decides to re-teach the content and give his students another opportunity to succeed.

Too often people remember the stress of an assessment and how a former teacher or two used testing as a punitive device. We hope through some of the examples in this chapter that we've reinforced that, assessment, regardless of the type, is really as much about improving instruction as it is about determining a student's current skills. Remember that CTE is a partnership between a teacher and a learner in many ways and assessment is another way to reinforce that relationship.

Tools for your toolbox

This chapter focuses on the benefits of assessment as a tool for improving instruction. It helps drive home the point that assessment isn't just about checking a student's knowledge, it's also about understanding the best way to "fine-tune" your own teaching ability. We have three examples in this chapter and the first one focuses on saving teacher time as well as using objective data from a third-party developed assessment.

My best advice for new CTE teachers is to save time by locating some of the excellent curriculum that's already been developed and is easy to access and use. Using already created curriculum units, lesson plans and assessments designed to inform and improve instruction whenever possible will save time as well as provide students carefully planned learning experiences.

Great examples for both new and veteran CTE teachers can be found on the free website: Transportation Careers: A Resource for Teachers (transportationcareers.org). Curriculum units and lesson plans are grouped together by themes, subject areas and grade levels and are aligned with national science standards as well as the Common Core State Standards in Mathematics and English Language Arts and Literacy in History/Social Studies, Science and related CTE Subjects.

The free materials include ideas for teacher assessment of student work as well as supplemental materials such as PowerPoint presentations and student handouts. Many of the modules on this free website are problem-based, using authentic industry problems for students to solve individually or in a group. All of the modules provide career information in Transportation, Distribution and Logistics Career Pathways, such as Transportation Operations, Logistics Planning and Management Services, Warehousing and Distribution Center Operations, Facility and Mobile Equipment Maintenance, Transportation Systems/Infrastructure Planning, Management and Regulation, Health, Safety and Environmental Management and Sales and Service. The assessments included provide new CTE teachers not only with a better understanding of their students' skills, but also the data they need to inform and improve their instruction.

We have some comments from a third-year Baking & Pastry Arts teacher that we think may be beneficial.

When students don't do well on tests, don't assume they are lazy. Always look in the mirror FIRST!

- Did you deliver the content correctly?
- Was your assessment designed well? Was the wording understandable?
- Did you receive feedback from your students regarding the quiz/test/exam?
- Were your expectations reasonable?
- Does the assessment *really* tell/show you evidence that the student understands the main ideas of the lesson?

As you acquire more experience in designing assessments, you may find that the results of multiple-choice or true/false tests are not informative enough. A student's odds of getting the answers correct on those kinds of tests might have been pretty good, so then the teacher still does not know if the students really *knew* the material. Continue to think creatively about designing new ways to test for student understanding.

I also started to adapt the way I give baking math assessments. The students do complete drills for basic baking knowledge on measurements. I'm working on new ways to test students. Many times, verbal assessments work much better than written math tests. My students do horribly with math/word problems. When they can "see" a problem, they can all generally solve the problem, especially when it applies directly to the hands-on portion of their work. I've noticed when I combine high content reading with basic math they become paralyzed, with the exception of a few students. The more I can separate math from reading, at least initially, the better they do and the more confident they become.

This chapter gave information about the importance of incorporating performance-based projects. Here is a brief sample from a child care teacher about the importance of establishing meaningful measures surrounding those projects.

We are CTE and naturally emphasize students working with their hands and tapping into their creative side. I wanted to create opportunities for my students that capitalized on their creativity and application of new skills. A longer-term type of project that I used successfully was a project that required my students to follow the letter recognition of the preschoolers that they were teaching in our laboratory preschool. High school students were responsible for collecting data and then graphing the data that exhibited upper case and lower case recognition in the beginning of the year and then again at the end of the year. They were also responsible for creating a parent workshop for the preschoolers they were working with to share ideas and lessons we completed at the school's lab to support early literacy skills.

Parent resource folders were created by the high school students which included sample lessons and easy-to-do activities at home with their preschoolers. High school students were also required to reflect on their lessons and the effectiveness and impact they had on the preschoolers in increasing their skills. Rubrics served as the guidelines for evaluating the project and were shared ahead of time so that students understood the expectations. Self-reflection allowed the high school students the opportunity to grow and develop their own individual teaching skills and show a bit of creativity in the process.

KEY LEARNINGS:

1. Testing is as much about instructional improvement as it is about student evaluation.
2. Incorporation of pretests, formative tests and summative tests is standard practice.
3. Standardized pretests and summative tests must be aligned to national industry expectations and local programs of study.
4. A grade is a symbol indicating a range of general technical competence.
5. Benchmarking is a valuable tool for both individual and classroom diagnosis of existing competence.
6. Unit tests and quizzes are tools to continually monitor teaching success and student retention.
7. Performance projects provide an opportunity for students to apply their skills.
8. Informal item analysis is a great way to diagnose progress of the teacher and the students.

RELATED CONTENT THAT MAY BE OF INTEREST:

Articles

Boudett, K. P., Murnane, R. J., City, E., & Moody, L. (2005). Teaching Educators: How to Use Student Assessment Data to Improve Instruction. *Phi Delta Kappan, 86(9)*, 700-706. (ERIC Number: EJ712938).

Cromey, A. (2000, November). *Using Student Assessment Data: What Can We Learn from Schools?* (Policy Issues Brief No. 6). Oakbrook, IL: National Central Regional Educational Laboratory. (ERIC Number: ED452593).

Educational Testing Service (2015). *How Tests and Test Questions are Developed*. Princeton, NJ: Author. Retrieved From: www.ets.org/understanding_testing/test_development/.

Ferlazzo, L. (2014, November 29). Formative Assessments are Powerful: Classroom Q&A with Larry Ferlazzo. *Education Week*. Retrieved from http://blogs.edweek.org/teachers/classroom_qa_with_larry_ferlazzo.

Foster, J., Hodes, C.L., & Pritz, S.G. (2014). Chapter VII: Analyzing the Data in *Putting Your Data to Work: Improving Instruction in CTE*. Alexandria, VA: ACTE.

Glazer, N. (2014). Formative Plus Summative Assessment in Large Undergraduate Courses: Why Both? *International Journal of Teaching and Learning in Higher Education*, 26(2), 276-286. (ERIC Number: EJ1060846).

Hattie, J. (2003). Formative and Summative Interpretations of Assessment Information. *Who Says Formative Assessment Matters?* Retrieved from www.scribd.com/doc/50784590/2003-Hattie-Formative-and-summative-interpretations-of-assessment-information#scribd.

Institute of Education Science. (2015). Designing Quasi-experiments: Meeting What Works Clearinghouse Standards Without Random Assignment (Webinar transcript). Washington DC: U.S. Department of Education. Retrieved from http://ies.ed.gov/ncee/wwc/multimedia.aspx?sid=23.

NOCTI (2015). Assessments, Blueprints. Big Rapids, MI: Author. Retrieved from www.nocti.org/Pre-Testing.cfm?m=2.

chapter VII
Connecting With Parents

Celebrations of successes can give students, as well as parents, a sense of pride as the students work to achieve the program of study (POS) goals. The power of celebration can motivate students to want to learn and achieve even more. However, the sharing of student successes should be an authentic means to recognize students' accomplishments and efforts rather than focusing on reward recognition systems. Celebrations can be big or small, private or public, one-on-one or in a group. Examples would be:

Can I post that on the fridge?

- Recognizing a student as your "Student of the Marking Period."
- Posting pictures of students and their accomplishments on your bulletin board or the school's.
- Recognizing your students' successes on your teacher or school web page.
- Taking some time to talk to the student about his or her progress and how proud you are of what they've accomplished.

- Posting your students' accomplishments in the school newsletter. If your student achieves a state or national accomplishment, a release in the local newspaper may be appropriate.

Celebrations should be personal, fun, consistent (happening often) and recorded in some way (informally or formally) (Fox, 2015).

Don't forget to communicate with parents about student celebrations, the very happiest kind of communication! Sending home a personal letter, phoning or sending an email or text to a parent can accomplish this—whatever method of communication is best for the parent. This chapter will focus on ways to establish positive parent communication, including beginning-of-the-year letters, parent-teacher meetings/conferences, documentation of student success, documentation (formal and informal) of student problems/concerns and follow-up responses and updates to parents.

Parental communication, interaction and support

What is one of the most underused resources in education today to help students to succeed? Parents! They can help increase student motivation, engagement and achievement and decrease a teacher's workload. Parental involvement is clearly linked with academic success for all students, regardless of income level (Barlis, 2013).

Establishing clear, ongoing lines of communication at the beginning of the school year helps establish positive interactions between the teacher

 and students' parents throughout the school year. Most often parents not only want to know what grades their student is receiving, but also generally how he or she is doing in the POS and if they are progressing appropriately to attain industry competency to continue to postsecondary education, if desired. Parents will also often want to be informed about school events so they may feel like part of the team in the education of their son or daughter.

Invite parents to check out your teacher webpage on the school's site, if applicable, to learn more about you, your POS, student expectations and ways to contact you.

Mariconda (2015) suggests five ground rules for effective communication with parents:

1. Begin the year by explaining to parents and students how and when you'll keep in touch with them (letters, emails, phone calls, meetings, etc.). Send home a welcome letter or newsletter that informs parents how you may be contacted and the time periods available. Consider electronic media and the school's website.
2. Never feel pressured to make an important decision, evaluation or assessment during a parent conference or conversation. If more time is needed (to consider the issue, develop possible solutions or consult with colleagues or administrators), let the parent know when to expect a response and how it will be communicated.
3. Let parents know they can trust you. You will not share private student information or concerns with others who do not need to know. This information is confidential. It is important to also emphasize your connection to the industry you represent. This increases your credibility.
4. Assure parents that you will inform them immediately about any concerns you might have with regard to their child. Parents may become extremely upset when the first sign of trouble comes in the form of a progress report halfway into the marking period or, even worse, with the report card grade.
5. When presenting a concern to parents, *always* be prepared to explain what strategies you've already used to address the issue and what new strategies you are considering, perhaps based on their input.

Halloran (2015) suggests seven parent-teacher communication tips that can help as well:

1. Set your objectives with the parents in mind as well as your students. Do you want to have better student attendance? Will you bring parents into the classroom to share professional experiences with students? Create a conversation with parents in order to further your objectives in the classroom.
2. Set and communicate clear, consistent and high expectations in your parent-teacher communication plan. Research has shown that parental expectations are one of the strongest predictors of student achievement. This will help to put parents on your side to enable them to reinforce your expectations in the home.
3. Communicate and often. If student expectations are communicated to parents early in the year, it is more likely that they will support you.

4. Communicate about the entire classroom as well as individual students. Make sure that parents are aware that you're responsible for more than just their student. This will hopefully help them to see your point of view better when you need to make a decision that is best for the group, yet might not be ideal for each student.
5. Be aware of school-wide communications. Parents will not only be hearing from you, but also from the school. They don't want to feel that only fundraising requests are being communicated to them.
6. Choose communication tools that work for parents. Ask them how they want you to contact them (e.g., phone calls, emails, texts).
7. Measure your success and pay attention to results. Are you getting parents engaged? Do they return signed permission slips? Does their child arrive prepared for class? Is the negative student behavior decreasing? Adapt the parent communication plan, if necessary.

Letters to parents

An introductory letter from you is a way of welcoming CTE students and parents to your program (Ritz, 2014). The tone of the letter should be very polite, but written formally and professionally. When creating this initial letter to parents, try to personalize the greeting instead of typing, "Dear Parents/Guardians." If possible, address them as Mr. and Mrs. (last name). Begin with a very positive first statement about the excitement of a new school year, the return of their son or daughter for another year in your program, if it is a multi-year program. Provide an introduction of yourself if the student is new to your program or if it is his or her first year with you. This could include where you grew up, went to school/college, your interests/hobbies and why you chose your technical profession and teaching. It is important to include a basic description of the program objectives, the materials that students will need to bring with them to class (shop clothing, personal tools or other items, etc.), classroom and shop expectations for student behavior and anything else that you feel is necessary to communicate to parents early in the school year. Follow this with ways the parents can contact you and the best times for that to occur. Let them know that you will do your best to keep them informed, not only of student concerns, but also of student successes. End the letter with another positive statement or two about looking forward to teaching their son or daughter. Do try to keep this letter to one or two pages at most. Ask your mentor or other veteran teachers if they are willing to share their beginning-of-the-school-year parental letters with you. You certainly can use their examples to guide and personalize your letter.

Some teachers also send an end-of-the-school-year letter to parents. Again, personalize the greeting as you did in the first letter. Focus on what major topics were taught during this school year; special events that occurred, such as technical competitions, field trips or speakers; provide feedback on what their child accomplished that year; what challenges he or she needs to continue to work on; and what things to look forward to in the next school year (if the student is not graduating). Try to keep the lines of communication open and positive between you, the parents and your students.

Parent-teacher meetings

Ms. Neuteach checks her email and she sees this message from XXXX: "Good morning. I would appreciate it if you could arrange to meet in the guidance office at 4 p.m. tomorrow for a parent-teacher meeting concerning your student, Joey Smith. Bring any notes that you may have about his behavior and be prepared to discuss concerns with his parents." She thinks, "I guess I should have expected this, but what do I bring with me, what should I think about in order to prepare for this discussion with his parents and will anyone else be with me or will I be all alone to face them? I haven't had a parent meeting before!" Don't worry. This scenario of meeting with students' parents is bound to happen, often sooner rather than later. Even if you haven't been proactive with parent communications, these kinds of meetings can be productive for all parties involved, but some preparation is needed.

One really important question to always ask when trying to correct and change an undesired student behavior is, "*Why* is this student acting this way?" If you know the answer to that question, hopefully you'll be able to understand the situation better and decide what changes or actions should be taken to resolve the problem. The corrective action plan should be shared not only with the student, but also with the parents. What happens at home between the student and his or her parents can, and often does, affect what happens in school. It may be something that you cannot change or control if it is occurring in the home environment, or you may need to contact other school personnel (such as an administrator or guidance counselor) if it is something serious. However, try to change what is within your power and remember that what works with one student may not work with others. Also ask fellow teachers for suggestions of how they correct similar problems with their students and then decide on your own plan of action. Share your basic expectations for student behavior with your students *and* their parents.

Whenever student problems occur, it is best to first talk one-on-one to the student privately; informally document (on a note card or student file) what was discussed, with the date noted. This ongoing record can be very helpful if the behavior does not change appropriately and quickly enough, or if it becomes necessary to contact an administrator and/or the parents. If a parent-teacher meeting is called, you should bring your record of what you have done so far to help the student correct the behavior or concern.

Your school may have printed forms available for you to record student behavior concerns formally (such as a student referral form, a detention form, etc.). The parent-teacher meeting is usually set in a neutral location, such as an administrator or guidance counselor's office with one or both parties present so you are not alone to face the parents. The meeting often begins on a positive note of welcome. Remember that parents may feel anxiety about meeting their student's teacher or feel frustration with the behavior of the child, so begin your portion of the conference with a positive statement regarding the student's positive qualities and strengths followed by your concern about the current problem to be addressed.

Next, you will provide your input (taken from your informal or formal documentation on the student) concerning the one-on-one discussions and corrective actions that have been taken to correct the issue thus far. Communication is a two-way street, so time should be given for the parents to respond to what they think they have heard and to ask questions for clarification. Together you should create a plan of action to help the student to correct the cause of the concern.

If the tone of the meeting should ever begin to become negative (raised voices, accusations, etc.) and not improve within a very brief period of time, then the meeting should end promptly. Once things cool down, another meeting date and time can be set. The good news is that these meetings rarely become negative, but usually are informative for all involved. A "team" plan involving the teacher, parents and others is sometimes much more effective than the teacher trying to deal with the student concern alone. Follow-up communication with the student and the parents should occur (in whatever form is appropriate) as soon as a positive change in behavior is observed. Catch the student being good (making the  positive changes in actions)! As soon as you see those positive changes, communicate that observation with the parents to reinforce improved behavior at home as well as at school.

Luckily Ms. Neuteach had a strong support system available to her. She didn't have to face parents alone and unprepared. She asked her peers to suggests ways of handling some of her more challenging student behavior problems (especially any concerning the safety of the individual student or others), ways to communicate effectively with students and parents, how to record information so as to keep accurate records of behavioral problems, and how to prepare for those occasional parent-teacher meetings. She soon learned that positive and open communication with parents usually results in resolving any student behavior problems quickly and effectively. For CTE teachers who often have students for longer than one school year, this parent-teacher contact can be one of the greatest assets in helping each student to progress through the POS.

Tools for your toolbox

Numerous online sources offer advice and examples for new teachers with regard to communication with parents. One example is a parent communication Log Template (2012) that is helpful for parent-teacher conferences; it is available at www.logtemplate.com/parent-communication-log.html. At the top of this template, the student's name and meeting date are recorded. The teacher is able to list ahead of time, the item or concerns to be discussed with the parents so as to focus and keep discussion on target. There is also space for those items that were discussed during the meeting. Another section of the log provides space to list the action(s) to be taken as a result of the parent and teacher discussion. Finally, the bottom of the form provides an area for the teacher and parents' signatures with dates. This log serves to prepare the teacher for the parent conference, to record what was discussed and when, feedback received from the parents and what actions were to be taken to remedy the student problem.

Templates are important organizers, but real experience is a great teacher too. Here's an example from a new CTE teacher in Georgia and what he learned.

The first time I ever communicated with one of my student's parent was shortly after I had just been hired. I had been hired to finish out the school year for a teacher that had left their district due to a promotion. I was coming from Corporate America and had never taught in an official classroom setting. Basically, I was "*green*"!

I was teaching an Introduction to Digital Technology class and we were learning HTML. I say 'we' because HTML was also new to me. I attempted to make everything simple and easy to understand. Unfortunately, I had a student that was not grasping the HTML concepts and his classroom behavior reflected that. I observed the student's negative behavior and even though he was more than capable of learning the information, he chose to focus on being a classroom distraction. I talked to the student after class on two occasions about his conduct and didn't see any improvement. This is when I decided to call his parents and see if his parents could assist me in getting this young man back on track.

I called the student's mother and explained that I needed assistance in helping her son to be successful in my class. I explained that her son was capable of successfully completing the work and how he should be one of my top students in class. The mother patiently listened as I explained the situation regarding her son's behavior and what I had done to try to correct it.

The mother then simply asked, "What can I do?" I was pleasantly surprised. She did not argue or try to deny the actions of her child, but simply asked ‹What can I do?› *I have heard the stories and read articles about parents not being involved or really not concerned about the education of their children, but this was not the case.* This mother really wanted to be involved and help establish some corrective actions. I gave her a few suggestions about classroom behavior to discuss with him and almost immediately saw an improvement. The student's parent and I communicated several times during the remainder of the school year to ensure the classroom success of her son.

This interaction taught me that a lot of parents really want to be actively involved, but they don't necessarily know how. It is sometimes the job of the educator to make those suggestions and help establish that success plan.

In all my parent communications I try to develop some type of improvement strategy before I talk to a student's parent. I want to communicate ways the student can overcome any sort of obstacles without hesitation. My objective is not to only communicate problems, but to also provide realistic solutions that may fall within my area of expertise. This process has really helped me when dealing with parents because it illustrates that I sincerely have the child›s best interest at heart and want to see them succeed in life.

Another example of a general chart to record parent-teacher communication (Winston, 2015) is available at www.teachingoasis.com/Parent%20Communication%20Log.pdf.

The following is a glimpse of what it looks like; its format can be used for additional parental contacts:

Parent Communication Log

Contact with (parent's name): _____

Concerning (student's name): _____

Date and Time of contact: _____

Reason for Contact: _____

_____

Notes and summary of discussion: _____

_____

_____

_____

Method of Contact:

- ☐ Phone
- ☐ Email
- ☐ Note or Text
- ☐ In Person

When contacting parents by phone or by email, this online source is also available from Priceless Teaching Strategies (2008) at www.priceless-teaching-strategies.com/parent_contact.html, which suggests:

1. Make contact early in the school year (using the beginning-of-the-school-year letter or newsletter) so that communication has already been established with the parents.
2. Parents must be notified if the student's problem has escalated and not been resolved.
3. You may choose to send an email or make a phone call to the parent if you believe that your letter to the parent was intercepted by the student.
4. At the beginning of the conversation, let the parent know that you are not calling about an emergency, but need time to discuss a concern regarding their child. Remember to begin the next part of the conversation with the strengths of the student (positive comments) before moving on to the area for improvement or your behavioral concern.

5. If you call the parent at a work number, be sure to ask if it is a good time to talk. If not, schedule another time to discuss the concern.
6. It's best not to call parents during your lunch or planning period, because the conversation may take longer than the time available.
7. You will probably want to refer to your notes so that you don't forget anything. Be sincere and specific. Don't raise too many issues at once so as not to overwhelm the parents.
8. Document the phone call or email and the main reason for it.
9. End the conversation on a peaceful and positive note by saying something to the effect of, "We need to work together in a partnership because we both want (student's name) to succeed."
10. Do follow up with communication to the parent in a timely fashion to review progress made by the student.
11. If the issue is still not resolved, speak to an administrator to arrange for a parent-teacher conference and/or to decide if further action is required by the school.
12. Finally, if contacting parents by email, do so using your school email address, not your personal email address.

As a final thought for this chapter on parent-teacher communication, remember this: A teacher is not only responsible for imparting knowledge to students, but also has a hand in developing and molding their attitude and personality. Because teachers are so involved in  the lives of their students, it is important for them to communicate with parents (Ritz, 2014).

KEY LEARNINGS:

1. Be positive and proactive with parents.
2. Make parents part of your instructional team.
3. Communicate often.
4. Assure that communication can occur in a variety of formats and is a two-way street.
5. Consider a beginning-of-the-school-year letter and an end of-the-school-year letter to parents.
6. Document student behavioral concerns and steps to correct them.
7. Prepare thoroughly for a formal meeting with parents.
8. Be objective, honest and professional in any communication.

RELATED CONTENT THAT MAY BE OF INTEREST:

Aguilar, E. (2014, November 3). *20 Tips for Developing Positive Relationships With Parents*. Jossey Bass Education. Available at http://josseybasseducation.com/teaching-learning/20-tips/.

Research & Innovation Network. (2015). *Stronger Communication*. Center for Learning Science & Technology. Available at http://researchnetwork.pearson.com/learning-science/teaching-in-a-digital-age/stronger-communication.

Ritz, G. (2014, September 16). *New CTE Teacher Resources: Parent Communications. Indiana Department of Education.* Available at www.doe.in.gov/cte/new-cte-teacher-resources.

Wayne Technical & Career Center. (2015). *Communicating the Value of CTE to Parents*. Available at www.waynetechcenter.org/parents.cfm?subpage=1352294.

chapter VIII
IEP Basics

"I just checked my class roster and one-third of my new students have IEPs. Now what do I do? I think IEP has something to do with special education. I'm not a special education teacher and I don't have any training on how to teach special education students. Frankly, I just started my college courses and I am learning how to teach. I need help!" Does this sound like something you may have said at the beginning of the school year?

CTE teachers entering their new profession directly from industry rarely possess any sort of special education certification and usually begin their teaching career with no preparation in special education. Fortunately, CTE teachers enter their teaching career with mastery-level knowledge and skills in their specific trade or occupation. They possess subject-matter expertise and have considerable experience working with a wide range of individuals of varying ability in their occupational specialty. In many cases, they have worked with and/or trained new or intern employees who have some type of disability and have witnessed those workers achieve proficiency in both

Everyone has skills right?

basic and advanced knowledge and higher-level skill development. CTE teachers bring to the classroom their personal experiences from working as part of a team of co-workers with a variety of skills and abilities. They are often successful in educating special needs students because of that experience. In addition, the CTE lab setting is a more supportive learning environment than the workplace. Unlike the workplace, instruction in a CTE lab is focused on the individual learning styles of students and not production schedules and profit margins.

The intent of the information in this chapter is to provide a basic knowledge of the CTE teacher's role and responsibilities in the Individualized Education Program (IEP) process and to help CTE teachers prepare and deliver effective instruction to students with disabilities.

Legal background

The nation's special education law is the Individuals with Disabilities Education Act or IDEA (http:// idea.ed.gov). IDEA establishes the

right of students with disabilities to a free appropriate public education, including special education, career technical education, support services and transition services. The Career and Technical Education Improvement Act of 2006 (also known as the Carl D. Perkins Career and Technical Education Act of 2006 (Public Law 109-270)), also requires focus on special populations, including students with disabilities, within CTE programs and services.

IDEA defines the term "child with a disability" and it includes 14 categories and definitions of disabilities. The disabilities listed include: autism; deaf-blindness; deafness; developmental delay; emotional disturbance; hearing impairment; intellectual disability; multiple disabilities; orthopedic impairment; other health impairment; specific learning disability; speech or language impairment; and traumatic brain injury and visual impairment, including blindness.

First, let's start with some basics. An IEP is a written statement of the educational program designed to meet the student's "unique" needs and abilities. Essentially, the IEP sets reasonable goals for the student and it details the services that will be provided by the school and its staff.

In brief, the IEP development process involves a group of people working together as a team that includes special education, CTE and regular education teachers, support staff, counselors and school administration, and the students' parents. The team may also include other education and healthcare professionals. The entire IEP process is focused on the individual student and it is driven by the student and his/her parents.

The process begins with an assessment of the individual student's interest, abilities, needs and preferences. The student's post-high school goals are also identified. Next, instructional activities, accommodations and supports are aligned to the student's post-high school goals. The IEP must include school and work-based activities that integrate high academic and workplace standards.

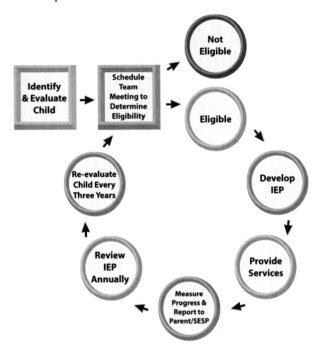

New CTE teachers may be required to provide a number of accommodations for special education students ranging from extending the amount of time on a test or skill performance and providing preferential seating in the classroom and/or an alternate note-taking method to conducting frequent checks for comprehension and/or providing assistance from an instructional assistant. CTE teachers are a critical part of the IEP development process because they can identify specific course or program prerequisites and an inventory of requisite entry-level occupational skills that would be helpful in developing the IEP.

A CTE program of study and a competency profile showing specific occupational tasks, the conditions under which they are performed and the industry standards for each task are important information essential to the development of an appropriate educational plan. A CTE teacher often participates in the IEP process and serves as a key member of the IEP team, especially when the determination is being made to place the student in a specific CTE program. The CTE teacher's subject-matter expertise is a valuable resource for goal setting and determining accommodations and support relevant to the student enrolling in the occupational program.

Prior to the first day of instruction

Before the first day of class, CTE teachers should be provided a copy of their students' IEPs and a meeting with the school's instructional support team (special education) should have been completed; if not, it should be scheduled as soon as possible. CTE teachers must be prepared to provide the appropriate support for each student from day one. The preparation begins with a discussion among the support team about the requirements in each IEP, the nature of accommodations and the support required by the teacher and/or other school staff.

The timing of just when a CTE teacher receives a copy of the students' IEPs and the subsequent meeting with the secondary or instructional support team is critical. New CTE teachers and teachers with only a few years of teaching experience should not wait to receive IEPs and help from the support team. Remember, every CTE program and every teacher in the school may have special education students with an IEP. There can be several hundred special education students in a school; new teachers need to be prepared to educate every child starting on day one. It could take several days or weeks until the school's instructional support team can schedule meetings with every teacher. New or second-year teachers should ask the supervisor to expedite a meeting with the school's instructional support team and seek additional advice from a veteran or a mentor teacher regarding how they prepare for and support special education students in CTE programs.

Typically, career and technical schools provide a list of recommended teaching techniques and teaching strategies and appropriate accommodations that will help CTE teachers provide effective instruction in support of the individual learning styles of students. In addition to the examples of accommodations provided previously, CTE teachers may be required to provide physical modifications to facilities and equipment, such as changing table heights and adaptations to equipment controls to provide greater accessibility. Knowing the support requirements in the IEP is the first step in preparation for instruction; providing the actual accommodations and support will ensure students are successful.

Benefits of CTE

High school students pursue CTE for a variety of reasons. In addition to CTE being the preferred choice for students seeking a career in a health, business, service or a technical occupation, special education students may benefit greatly from the teaching styles, contextual basis and "hands-on learning" inherent in CTE. In many cases, the IEP process and the IEP team will determine the student's placement or enrollment in CTE. You will also find those students who have expressed their desire to participate in a specific occupation years before the IEP determined that CTE was the appropriate placement. These students want to be enrolled in CTE and they are highly focused because they have a career goal. They are motivated and want to do well in the CTE program of their choice. They are not enrolled as a result of a "default" placement. Their interest and abilities helped the IEP team determine the student's participation in a specific CTE program, which is the primary reason they are enrolled.

Research shows that students with disabilities gain a direct benefit from participation in CTE. The National Longitudinal Transition Survey 2 (NLTS2) data shows that approximately 60 percent of youth with disabilities hold jobs at some time during high school and gain valuable experience in the world of work (Newman, Wagner, Huang, Shaver, Knokey, Yu, Contreras, Ferguson, Greene, Nagle, & Cameto, 2011). The NLTS2 findings showed that students who were enrolled in CTE were significantly more likely than nonparticipants to do well on school and post-school outcomes. The students in the survey had significantly lower absenteeism from school and a lower probability of dropping out of school. CTE training was related to a higher likelihood of finding a paid job and attending a postsecondary CTE school in the early years after high school (Newman, Wagner, Knokey, Marder, Nagle, Shaver, Wei, with Cameto, Contreras, Ferguson, Greene, & Schwarting, 2011).

Newman, Wagner, Huang, et al. (2011) also documented that students with disabilities improve their academic achievement as a result of the integrated academic and CTE curriculum, and they are more likely to be employed in the occupation of their CTE concentration. Students with disabilities enjoy other benefits from participation in CTE such as improved motivation, self-esteem and self-actualization. CTE provides the pathway for the fulfillment of their post-school goals.

CTE is not special education, but students with disabilities learn exceptionally well in CTE programs due to the contextual nature of the applied and differentiated learning activities and the relevance to the career interests of students (Castellano, Sundell, Overman & Aliaga, 2012). Effective teaching strategies include: setting high expectations and demonstrating caring for the student as an individual, using small-group and individualized instruction or differentiated instruction, student-to-student or peer coaching and computer-based or online blended learning. These are just a few successful strategies for teaching every CTE student, not just students with disabilities.

Differentiated instruction and CTE

Not surprisingly, special education teachers are highly skilled in teaching special education students. They are experts in providing instruction in a manner that supports the different learning styles of special education students (Sparks, 2015). In addition to years of classroom experience, special education teachers have mastered their instruction through pre-service preparation in college. They routinely participate in professional development activities, benefiting from the latest research on learning and advances in technology. Special education teachers are an excellent resource for CTE teachers in planning and delivering individualized or differentiated instruction.

Similar to special education, CTE teachers commonly employ individualized instruction techniques in the classroom and lab. The very nature of standards or competency-based instruction lends itself to differentiated instruction. CTE teachers routinely provide one-on-one instruction to every student who needs clarification and/or additional help. CTE teachers do it intuitively because many occupations have been taught for centuries by a master craftsman teaching an apprentice. Many CTE teachers learned their trade through one-on-one or individualized instruction and mentoring from a journeyman or master technician.

Hear it, see it, do it!

Much has been written about differentiated instruction and it would be difficult to address all of the various components that contribute to the concept. Differentiated instruction applies to every level of instruction from elementary education to graduate school, including academic, special education and CTE. A working definition for differentiated instruction in CTE is a teaching strategy that matches the individual learning styles of students with their interests and abilities. The teaching strategies may vary from student to student or between groups of students, but the essence of differentiated instruction is making the instruction relevant to the individual student. Relevance in CTE can be achieved by connecting instruction to the occupation and the prior learning experiences of students. In essence, CTE teachers personalize instruction to students' interests and differences.

CTE curriculum (what we teach) is based on a program of study that contains an occupational analysis. An occupational analysis has several components, but two elements that provide the basic framework for CTE curriculum and instruction are the *job titles* or career ladder and the *tasks or competencies* performed within the occupation. The occupational analysis makes CTE curriculum well suited for differentiated instruction (how we teach). The competency-based method of defining the CTE curriculum and delivering instruction provides an excellent framework for instruction that is easily aligned to the IEP process and highly supportive in goal setting and identifying supportive accommodations for students with disabilities.

Most CTE teachers usually begin instruction by teaching theory in a classroom on a major area or system within the occupational program. The instruction provides the theoretical knowledge of the occupational component so that students can understand the "how and why" of the system, including how it works and its relationship to the other major components of the occupation. The knowledge will enable students to analyze and comprehend the processes and/or products developed during the practical application phase of instruction. In other words, when students understand the science and technologies behind the occupational component, they can connect the theoretical to the practical application and achieve higher skill levels in the performance of tasks in their chosen profession. Relevance links the theoretical and the task performance.

The basic element of a CTE curriculum is the task or competency. A task has three components: the *task* statement or what is to be performed, such as "replace brake lining"; the *conditions* under which the task is performed, such as "with the use of a technical repair manual" or "locate the manufacturer's repair procedures online"; and the *standard* or degree of accuracy to which the task must be performed, in this example "to 100 percent accuracy as defined by manufacturer specifications." Obviously, 90 or 95 percent accuracy would not be acceptable for a safety repair on automobile brakes. In other instances, a plus or minus standard on a measurement or a lower percentage may be acceptable. Standards may vary by the nature of the task and occupation, but business and industry determine the standards, not educators.

The *task* or competency and the *standard* for accuracy are required by business and industry and for employment; the task and standard cannot be changed to accommodate various learning styles of students with disabilities. The *conditions* under which the task is performed generally follows the conditions under which the task is performed in the workplace. However, the conditions in the educational setting (CTE lab) can be modified to accommodate the individual needs of students with disabilities; providing guided practice during the hands-on performance component of instruction gives additional support to the student. Some students may perform the procedure or prepare a product to the expected standards on one attempt; other students may require several attempts (Guskey

& Anderman, 2014). One or more steps in the procedure may have to be repeated until the standard is obtained. Providing varying levels of guided practice aligned to the needs and abilities of each student is an effective differentiated instructional method.

Accommodations in the classroom and lab may be similar, or they can vary based on the setting and the student's abilities. Some students may need more support to learn the theoretical content, others may need additional support in the hands-on performance component of the CTE program, and some students may need both accommodations. Ultimately, student performance in the lab setting must include safety and proficiency to the standard on the tasks or competencies associated with the student's career or post-school goal.

There may be times when CTE teachers must teach a unit of instruction to the entire class, but routinely keeping students in a large group and instructing them on the same theory and tasks is an inappropriate teaching strategy. That would be teacher-centered instruction, the least desired method of teaching CTE students, especially students with learning disabilities. In teacher-centered curriculum and instruction, the curriculum is written in a way that brings focus to the teacher as the sole source of learning. During teacher-centered instruction, the students rely on the teacher for resources and the learning pace is controlled by the teacher. For some teachers, teacher-centered curriculum and instruction may be easier than facilitating individual student learning activities and providing differentiated instruction. However, teacher-centered instruction does not support the individual learning styles and needs of students. It sets low expectations and discourages student-initiated learning. Teacher-centered instruction is addressed in this chapter because it is practiced by some CTE teachers, but it is an ineffective practice, particularly when working with students with diverse needs.

In reality, CTE instructors routinely provide individualized instruction to CTE students because every student learns and masters skill performance at his or her own pace. Individualized and student-centered instruction is differentiated instruction (Moyer, 2015). Encouraging students to become self-directed learners establishes high expectations for students and it allows them to learn as individuals (Guskey & Anderman, 2014). Self-directed learning is student-centered learning and it establishes a learning environment that enables the teacher to spend more time supporting students with disabilities. The concept of student-centered curriculum and instruction does require greater preparation by the teacher in developing learning materials (learning guides or learning activity packets) that enable students to become self-directed learners. Students can locate the instructional materials and resources necessary to progress from unit to unit of instruction and from task to task with minimal assistance from the teacher. The teacher becomes a learning facilitator and instructs students in small groups or individually.

CTE teachers often use other students to help students learn. They can provide student-to-student coaching or they can work in a team to analyze and perform service or repair tasks. Assigning an upper level or advanced student with a student that may need extra help reinforces the learning for the advanced student and allows the less knowledgeable student to learn from another class member in a manner that promotes teamwork. The teacher can recognize the accomplishments of the team and the individual team members. It builds a student's self-confidence and it is a highly effective teaching strategy.

Other effective differentiated instructional strategies that move learning beyond the school setting include computer-aided and online-blended  learning. Providing work-based learning activities such as job shadowing, internships, paid work experience and a work-site mentor allows students to apply the skills and knowledge in the world of work.

Obviously, some teaching strategies are more effective than others, but experienced CTE teachers have learned that the most effective strategies for educating students with disabilities are also the most effective strategies for educating all CTE students. Every student has skills—providing individualized or differentiated instruction is what CTE teachers do best.

CTE teachers must continue to learn new teaching strategies and what works best for students in their instructional setting. Continued professional development is the best way to learn about the latest research on how students learn and the latest teaching methods that enhance educational achievement for all students.

The most important and effective accommodation that can be provided to students with disabilities is the personal and professional support provided by the CTE teacher. CTE teachers mentor students, provide support, engage, encourage and set high expectations for all students. Helping students with disabilities to be successful in CTE is part of an educator's ethical and professional responsibilities.

Tools for your toolbox

Our first reflection comes to us from a special needs teacher in Michigan and addresses the importance of individualizing instruction for all students.

As stated in IDEA, an IEP is designed to meet a student's individual needs and abilities, but as we think about our class, don't all of our students have unique needs and abilities? Of course they do. If we truly want to apply the whole child pedagogical model to our classrooms, we should look at the IEP process and apply a scaled-down version to all of our students. While it wouldn't be feasible to conduct a full-fledged IEP for each of our students, we can still utilize the essential elements of an IEP to help ensure that all students reach their highest potential. As a teacher, I focus on three main components of the IEP process (annual goals, supports and accommodations and transition services) and implement them under the premise of Universal Design for Learning (UDL). The notion is that what is beneficial for some will be beneficial for everyone.

All educators are an integral part of helping students reach their potential, but they first need to know for what they are reaching. Regardless of placement in CTE and regardless of the presence of a disability, all students should be focused on their future and what they hope to accomplish; all students should have goals. As part of my yearly instructional planning, I begin each school year by having students write SMART (Specific, Measurable, Attainable, Relevant, Time Bound) goals and action plans describing the steps they will need to take to reach these goals. Throughout the year, we revisit these goals and action plans to evaluate where they are in the process.

Accommodations are an important aspect of the IEP process, as many times changes need to be made to the curriculum and/or classroom setting. Yet, as we take a step back and look at these changes, we often find that they are also beneficial to a majority of students. It is important to remember that if a student does not have a disability, he or she can still benefit from the accommodations that have been implemented in an IEP. Many of the accommodations that are provided through an IEP can be implemented for an entire class. If an accommodation can help a student with a disability, there is a good chance that the same accommodation can help other students in the class.

Due to the nature of CTE, all students with an IEP should have a postsecondary transition plan in place. This plan should not only address the student's postsecondary goals for transitioning into the workforce or postsecondary education, but also address the skills that the student needs to be successful after high school. As instructors, we play a pivotal role in this planning.

CTE instructors typically deliver process-driven instruction; this means that the process is driven by standards that exist in a particular technical field. There is usually a conventional way to perform the process so that the results are of a consistent high quality. However, every now and then CTE teachers need to think of solutions outside the conventional processes so that they can meet the individual needs of an IEP student. Here is an example from a construction teacher of one simple, yet unconventional, way to solve a problem.

I remember that when Billy appeared in my first-year construction class, he seemed like any other student and he was very interested in learning to build homes. He participated actively in class and performed most basic hand-tool skills on the shop floor pretty well. You can imagine my surprise when I found out Billy had an IEP! Although I don't remember the specific name of the learning disorder, I think it was a form of dyscalculia. Billy had difficulty understanding the divisions on a measuring tool and converting the divisions of an inch into fractions. Billy understood the small marks if he could count them. He knew one little mark was one-sixteenth, the second little mark was two- sixteenths, yet he didn't understand that two-sixteenths was also one-eighth. As it turned out, a number of students had some difficulty with this. We started trying a couple of ideas for solutions in the classroom. We would show sections of rulers with a line on them and ask students to identify the length of the line. Sometimes we even made it part of a team competition. This helped not only Billy but also many of his classmates. The other idea we tried was to provide Billy with a "special" ruler we made up, which simply had the divisions of the first inch of the ruler written on it. The divisions were written with the lowest common denominator (1/4 as opposed to 4/16). Pretty soon we started to reduce Billy's dependence on the special ruler by letting him use it only on certain days, such as Mondays or the day after a vacation. I never knew whether Billy's understanding lasted in the years after he graduated, but his "special" ruler certainly helped him for the short-term. The experience made me realize that I could make some pretty basic changes that could improve my students' chances for success.

Another example from the Arkansas Career Training Institute provides an instructional accommodation based on a student's individual needs. This accommodation assisted the student to accomplish the same work and meet the same outcome goals as that of her peers.

Amanda's disability was dyslexia. The content of the Certified Nursing Assistant curriculum in which she was involved required reading large quantities of information with a challenging vocabulary. Amanda's disability made working through the curriculum and subsequent testing difficult. The accommodation made for Amanda included providing access to text-to-speech software, opportunities for audible reading of the material and extended time for testing. These accommodations were very successful and the outcome for Amanda was solid academic performance, outstanding development of hands-on skills and national recognition of her expertise and skills.

Amanda was able to graduate with an 87% cumulative GPA and passed both her written and practicum CNA licensure exams without issue. Amanda won a bronze medal at the HOSA State Competition in Health Occupations Portfolio with no accommodation made for her disability. At nationals, there was the opportunity to have the assistance of a test reader. The accommodation helped her do better, resulting in her bringing home a national title and placing 2nd in the nation, winning a silver medal.

These two examples not only served to help students overcome their particular disability, but they also helped open the teacher's mind to find simple, creative solutions that might work as a guide for students having similar difficulties.

For those of you working with adult populations, we provide another success story from Arkansas. This one, however, discusses physical adaptation; in fact, this one even required a complete career retooling.

Stewart worked in the transportation industry with a company that transports goods on the Arkansas and Mississippi Rivers. While working in this occupation, he had a traumatic injury to his left leg. Complications from the injury resulted in an amputation of his leg just below the knee. Because of this disability, he was no longer able to work on barges and in that sector of the transportation industry.

Stewart indicated he was interested in welding, and after a comprehensive evaluation of Stewart's strength, mobility, and aptitude, recommendations for a prosthesis and targeted physical therapy were made. During training Stewart was given short breaks during the hands-on training to help him develop his strength more gradually.

These accommodations were incorporated into a training plan that helped Stewart learn the skills of a welder and develop the physical skills involved in using his prosthesis effectively. The plan also involved monitoring his leg to avoid complications related to the amputation.

Stewart excelled in his training despite the fact that he had weekly physical therapy appointments and follow-ups with physicians; he finished his welding program on time and excelled both academically and in his hands-on skills. Prior to graduation, he was given the opportunity to interview for a position with High-Tech Engineering and was hired immediately upon graduation. Because of his skill level and his work ethic, he was chosen to go overseas to Australia to work with the company and serve as one of the lead welders on a construction project for a saw mill.

This example not only served to help the student overcome his particular disability, it also opened the teacher's mind to finding simple creative solutions that might work as a sort of guide or memorization tool for students having similar difficulties.

Our last example from a STEM teacher in Pennsylvania illustrates her experiences when accommodating a physical disability. This reflection takes place in a lab environment but could be applied to any CTE setting.

One of the more challenging classes over the years was a class of 29 students, one of which was hearing impaired. It was the first time that another adult was present in my classroom each day to sign what I said to the hearing-impaired student. I learned to slow down my speaking so that the interpreter had time to sign to him and also to learn if he had questions to ask of me. I ordered audiovisuals that included closed captions whenever possible.

It became even more interesting that school year when I learned that a visually impaired student was going to be added to that class in November. It was already challenging to rewrite classroom resources, but to learn that I would need to have these materials prepared at least two weeks before use so that they could be brailed was very difficult, but I managed to do it. That year, I had to think seriously about how to modify any hands-on activities so that both special needs students would be able to actively engage as the other students were expected to do.

One of the students in that class asked to be placed with the two special needs students during the hands-on activities. Although I kept an especially watchful eye on this group, I was so pleased to see that they worked very well together and completed tasks on time. I even heard other students comment that they were amazed at what the hearing and visually impaired students accomplished with very limited assistance from me. Knowing that I was closely examining, reflecting and rewriting portions of my lessons to be sure that I incorporated as many visual, auditory and tactile strategies as was practical really helped me.

I truly believe that all of my students benefitted from the modifications as did the two with IEPs. It seemed to be a win-win for everybody and I felt that I was a better educator because of that year's experience.

KEY LEARNINGS:

1. Students with special needs will end up as part of your CTE class.
2. The Individuals with Disabilities in Education Act mandates that students receive a free and appropriate education.
3. The CTE teacher must help to develop a student's IEP and should plan for its implementation.
4. Because of the "hands-on" environment in CTE classrooms, many students with special needs tend to be more successful.
5. Individualized instruction is very similar in concept to differentiated instruction.
6. Take time to analyze the component parts of the occupational pathway you are teaching; those skills help individualize instruction.
7. Ask the advice of experts, peers and mentors if you need methods to accommodate a student's instructional needs.

RELATED CONTENT THAT MAY BE OF INTEREST:

Articles

Castellano, M., Sundell, K., Overman, L. T., & Aliaga, O. A. (2012). Do Career and Technical Education Programs of Study Improve Student Achievement? Preliminary Analyses from a Rigorous Longitudinal Study. *International Journal of Educational Reform, (21)*, 98-118. Available at www.nrccte.org/resources/external-reports/do-career-and-technical-education-programs-study-improve-student.

Dolan, L., Ford, C., Newton, V., & Kellam, S. G. (1989). *The Mastery Learning Manual*. Johns Hopkins Center for Prevention and Early Intervention. Available at www.jhsph.edu/research/centers-and-institutes/johns-hopkins-center-for-prevention-and-early-intervention/Publications/mlm.pdf.

Guskey, T.R. & Anderman, E. (2014). In Search of a Useful Definition of Mastery. *Educational Leadership, 71*(4) 18-23. Available at www.be.wednet.edu/cms/lib2/WA01001601/Centricity/Domain/18/In%20Search%20of%20a%20Useful%20Definition%20of%20Mastery.pdf.

Individuals with Disabilities Education Act (IDEA). Available at http://idea.ed.gov/explore/home and www.disability.gov/individuals-disabilities-education-act-idea/.

Moyer, L. (2015). Begin With the End in Mind. ACTE blog. Available at www.acteonline.org/eia.post.aspx?id=4056&blogid=2666#.Vb_rxvnvfh4.

Newman, L., Wagner, M., Huang, T., Shaver, D., Knokey, A.-M., Yu, J., Contreras, E., Ferguson, K., Greene, S., Nagle, K., & Cameto, R. (2011). Secondary School Programs and Performance of Students With Disabilities. A Special Topic Report of Findings from the National Longitudinal Transition Study-2 (NLTS2). (NCSER 2012-3000). U.S. Department of Education. Washington, DC: National Center for Special Education Research. Available at http://ies.ed.gov/ncser/pubs/20123000/pdf/20123000.pdf.

Newman, L., Wagner, M., Knokey, A.-M., Marder, C., Nagle, K., Shaver, D., Wei, X., with Cameto, R., Contreras, E., Ferguson, K., Greene, S., & Schwarting, M. (2011). The Post-High School Outcomes of Young Adults with Disabilities up to Eight Years After High School. A Report From the National Longitudinal Transition Study-2 (NLTS2) (NCSER 2011-3005). Menlo Park, CA: SRI International. Available at http://ies.ed.gov/ncser/pubs/20113005/pdf/20113005.pdf.

Sparks, S. (2015, January 28). Differentiated instruction: A Primer. *Education Week*. Available at www.edweek.org/ew/articles/2015/01/28/differentiated-instruction-a-primer.html.

The Carl D. Perkins Career and Technical Education Act of 2006 (Public Law 109-270)). Available at www2.ed.gov/policy/sectech/leg/perkins/index.html.

chapter IX

Connecting with Occupational Advisory Committees

Do you have a not-so secret weapon?

"I really want to start my teaching career right! I know my trade and I am a master technician and now, I want to be a master teacher. I have a mentor teacher who is working with me, coaching me through the day-to-day activities and the new things I need to learn about the school and its policies and procedures. I have my first occupational advisory committee meeting next month and I want to make sure I am ready."

Since the early days of vocational education, external business and industry groups and employers have played a vital role in various aspects of the design and delivery of vocational technical instructional programs. The early federal Vocational Education Act of 1963 and subsequent amendments identified and strengthened the role of business and industry advisement in what is now known as CTE.

CTE is constantly changing due to emerging technologies, new processes, new equipment and product developments in business and industry. CTE educators must keep pace with the changes in the workplace; they rely on business and industry leaders and other SMEs to advise their school and teachers on a wide range of CTE issues. Unfortunately, many CTE educators do not maximize the full potential of business and industry advisory committees. They often fail to recruit enough master technicians and/or business owners and/or they do not engage the advisory committee for input on critical aspects of CTE program improvement.

In general, school districts, CTE schools and colleges utilize a two-tiered advisory structure. The top tier, or executive council, is composed of community leaders from business, secondary and postsecondary education, government, organized labor and workforce and economic development agencies. The top-tier advisory council focuses on visioning, CTE programming and school-wide or district-wide initiatives, such as funding and strategic planning.  The role of the executive-level advisory council is paramount to the future direction and programming of the organization. As a new teacher, you will probably have little interaction with this tier, but you should be aware of it.

The second tier provides individual occupational advisory committees (OACs) for each occupational program or CTE cluster. OAC is a term found in federal legislation, but there may be locally developed titles for these groups. Regardless of their specific title, the membership of the OAC reflects the composition of the occupation itself. The OAC is composed of master-level technicians, first-line supervisors and managers that

 possess subject matter expertise in the CTE field or occupation. The focus of OACs ranges from curriculum, facilities, equipment, industry certifications and credentialing, safety, occupational trends, student placement and student and program assessment. In addition, OAC members conduct the hands-on component of various certification performance assessments (like those offered by NOCTI), and they provide feedback on students' and recent graduates' performance on the job. OAC members serve other functions too, such as assisting in student and teacher recruitment; they can also serve as a source of technical professional development for teachers.

Typically, schools and colleges that deliver quality CTE programs maintain continual engagement with their business partners, most also host a minimum of two advisory committee meetings each year, perhaps a dinner meeting held in the fall and one in the spring. The agendas for the meetings sometimes begin with a general session in which the school leaders address major issues concerning the school and programs in general. After the opening session, individual occupational committee meetings are held. Unfortunately, this schedule greatly limits school leaders' participation in individual OAC meetings due to the large number of those meetings. A better approach is to schedule OAC meetings by cluster on one or two evenings per cluster, which will enable school leaders to be present at every OAC meeting. This approach allows leaders to address issues as they arise, rather than providing answers at a later date or at the next meeting in six months.

The names of the advisory committees often vary from state to state and sometimes even across schools or colleges. In the following descriptions of how each committee works, a new teacher will be able to identify the committee by its function regardless of what it may be called locally.

Local Advisory Committee (General Advisory)

The Local Advisory Committee (LAC) may be a standing committee of the school or school district. This committee acts as a link between the career center or school district and business and industry, postsecondary education, community and governmental entities. The LAC provides overall advice on program offerings, long-range plans and support services to aid college and career readiness.

The LAC should be comprised of recognized leaders of business, industry, organized labor, the local workforce investment board, economic development agencies, the public sector, community-based organizations, postsecondary education and recommended members of the community at large. Local school leaders often appoint members of an LAC for a specific term. The career center or school board should approve the LAC members to perform the duties of the LAC and Participatory Planning Committees. The council should meet a minimum of two times per year and should be convened by the LAC chairperson. The school superintendent and director of the school should serve on the leadership team of the LAC.

State departments of education or public instruction recommend the establishment of LACs and OACs. The following outline provides an overview of the structure and general responsibilities of the two-tiered advisory councils.

Local Advisory Committee

LACs provide broad direction for CTE programs, helping to reinforce the need for CTE program quality and access as well as:

- Support/strengthen the relationship among business, college, community and public education.
- Make recommendations on new or expanded areas of regional workforce and economic development growth around which programs should be developed.
- Assist in identifying needs, determining priorities and reviewing and evaluating programs; including state and federal grants.
- Perform the functions of the Carl D. Perkins Participatory Planning Committee.
- Promote state and local initiatives that will strengthen and identify human, technical and financial resources in support of CTE programs.
- Provide guidance around programs of study (POS) within the specific industry clusters and CTE programs.
- Provide guidance for articulation agreements and dual credit options within the specific career and technical programs.
- Advise on marketing and communicating the program to the community.
- Facilitate securing industry-specific resources.
- Recommend SMEs to serve on CTE occupational advisory committees.

Some colleges, career centers and/or school districts operate a separate Perkins-related planning committee. Its primary purpose is to ensure the school is planning educational activities and spending federal monies in support of the Perkins Act and state plan. In general, this is a district- or college-level committee, but in some instances the school leadership may ask a CTE teacher representative to serve on such a committee.

Industry Cluster Advisory Committees

The Industry Cluster Advisory Committee is similar to the OAC in its composition and responsibilities. Some career technical schools organize their advisory committees by industry cluster rather than by specific occupations, such as a Construction Cluster or an Automotive, Healthcare, Service or Manufacturing Cluster. The major goals are often the same or similar and are described below.

Occupational Advisory Committees

The purpose of OAC is to provide advice on CTE-specific occupations and program areas. The committees strengthen CTE by providing technical assistance at the building and individual program level. OACs work with CTE leaders and technical instructor(s) on the improvement of their program. The LAC, school administration and staff and community members can identify committee members. Committee members should possess current subject-matter expertise. Meetings should be held twice each year, at a minimum. The OACs are usually required by state regulations governing CTE and as part of a career center or school district's policies. Most states' department of education or public instruction issue guidelines for organizing and conducting occupational advisory committee meetings within the state. An efficient career center or school district usually provides brochures and membership application forms for OAC members.

The OAC is the business and industry partner of the school and teacher in helping the CTE program remain current with the expectations of local industry. The advisory committee members want and need the school and CTE teacher to be successful, because the school is their primary source of new employees. When CTE graduates enter the workplace properly prepared with recognized industry credentials, employers (advisory committee members) enjoy the benefit of highly productive workers and greater profits. When employers do not have access to highly trained CTE graduates, they spend a lot of time and money finding, screening and training new employees. Many employers serve on CTE advisory committees because they want to help shape the education and preparation of their future workers and they want access to CTE cooperative education students and program graduates. They rely on CTE teachers for the development of future workers and, in many cases, to provide the advanced skill training for their incumbent workers.

The authors note that the level of effectiveness of OACs varies greatly from state to state, from school to school, and often among CTE programs within a school. The quality of CTE is directly related to the level of business and industry engagement and the quality of the OAC membership and its role in program advisement. As a new teacher, you need to remember that your engagement doesn't end with the students and that classroom. Make it your goal to develop an OAC that builds ownership and greater levels of support for CTE, the school, CTE programs and CTE graduates.

A strategy that is common among schools that are highly successful in engaging their OACs is to conduct a special dinner meeting with OAC members. Hosting a dinner meeting at the career center will allow advisory members to come directly from work and feel appreciated that the school and its staff are sensitive to their time, plus it gives them an opportunity to see more of the school. Some CTE teachers have been successful in engaging OAC members by asking them if they would host a meeting at one of their business locations, at a trade association meeting or at the local community/technical college.

At least one meeting each year should involve a visit to the CTE lab because the occupational advisory committee needs to review the lab and instructional area for safety concerns, equipment suitability and the design or layout of the lab. Engaging OAC members in facility and equipment assessment and in the accreditation process for industry credentialing also builds greater industry support.

In terms of process, a critical point to remember is that the OAC chairperson runs the meeting and the CTE teacher is the facilitator, responsible for coordinating the logistics for the meeting and implementing the recommendations. Reporting back to OAC members in a timely manner on all recommendations, even if one or more recommendations are not feasible, reinforces the importance of the role of OAC members. Advisory committee members will resign or stop attending meetings if they feel they are making the same recommendations every year and little or no action is taken on their recommendations.

CTE teachers need to follow up on recommendations for equipment and do research on various brands, models and prices of the equipment recommended by the OAC. Teachers should prepare and submit all purchase requests in a timely manner. They must also prepare facility maintenance or modification requests in support of advisory committee recommendations. Being embarrassed at the next advisory committee meeting by a lack of action and follow-up damages not only your reputation, but that of your school as well. Failure to act on advisory committee recommendations is the fastest way to lose advisory committee support for CTE, the school and the program.

During one of the annual meetings, the OAC should review the benefits of providing industry credentials and other third-party assessments, the assessment process and their role in administering the hands-on performance component of NOCTI and other credentialing assessments. Teachers should share school and student achievement goals and test profile data with their OAC members. If business partners are helping with the assessment process on the day of a performance assessment, the CTE teacher should provide a brief review of procedures and requirements for OAC members to ensure everyone is prepared for their role in the test's administration. After the results of an assessment (data) are received, it is highly beneficial to engage OAC members in analyzing assessment data and in developing action plans for CTE program improvement.

Don't forget to involve OAC members in student recognition or graduation ceremonies and in career fairs at the school or college. Their presence  and supportive comments about students, the school and the program validate the importance of CTE. Asking OAC members to present industry certificates at graduation and/or senior awards ceremonies enhances the connections between CTE programs and local employers, while strengthening the engagement of advisory committee members. Involving OAC members in activities outside of school, such as asking them to invite current and future students and their parents to attend an open house at the OAC members' place of business, is another strategy that validates the relevance of CTE as a career choice and, once again, it strengthens the relationship between the school and employers. CTE teachers can recognize OAC members with a certificate of appreciation at OAC meetings; teachers can request special recognition for exceptional service by OAC members at school board meetings. Encouraging OAC members to ask program graduates and students who are seeking employment for a copy of their NOCTI certificate or other end-of-program assessment and/or industry certificate emphasizes the relevance of CTE and the world of work. When employers ask for CTE certificates, it adds significant value to the credential and it validates the efforts of OAC members and their participation in the assessment and school improvement process.

Personal contact between the CTE instructor and OAC members is the best strategy to build support for CTE and specific programs. Personal contact via a phone call, email message and a brief visit to the advisory committee member's place of business shows sincerity and appreciation for the OAC member's service on the committee. A follow-up visit by the CTE instructor to a few OAC members that employ students (e.g., via co-op) to talk to a supervisor about CTE students' progress, provides direct feedback about the program and student performance. Also, talking to co-op students and recent graduates enables the instructor to find out if they felt they were adequately prepared for the job, or would recommend an additional or different focus to the curriculum. Making personal contact with advisory committee members and program graduates is a highly effective engagement strategy.

In summary, schools and CTE teachers can increase business and industry engagement in CTE by involving OAC members in assessing student performance, sharing data and involving business and industry advisors as CTE stakeholders in the school and CTE program improvement process. School districts, colleges and CTE teachers must provide public recognition and show appreciation for OAC members' time and expertise.

Tools for your toolbox

This chapter discusses the importance and implementation of a variety of committees emphasized by the Perkins legislation. In this "Tools" section we have provided a few assessments, templates and, of course, a new teacher reflection that we hope you'll find useful. Let's start with the advisory committee effectiveness assessment.

The quality and relevance of CTE is highly dependent on advice from business and industry leaders and occupational subject matter experts. The quality of the advice provided by advisory committees is sometimes impacted by the organization of that committee, its membership and the program of work in which it is engaged (level of engagement).

Like CTE programs, the role and effectiveness of the advisory committee must be reviewed periodically. The committee must determine if it is accomplishing its goals and the extent to which its recommendations and actions are strengthening and improving the career and technical education program.

The assessment of the advisory committee's effectiveness should be conducted annually as an agenda item for the final meeting of the school year. Before CTE educators begin evaluating their advisory committee's effectiveness, they should determine if the school has a specific form and/or process for conducting an advisory committee effectiveness assessment. The reasons for conducting the effectiveness assessment must be reviewed with the advisory committee members and included at the end of the agenda for the last meeting of the school year. CTE school administrators should conduct the advisory committee effectiveness assessment; however, in the event that they do not conduct the assessment, CTE teachers should conduct their own informal assessment. The chairperson of the OAC can conduct the assessment and share the findings with the CTE teacher(s).

The following questions adapted from the Nebraska Department of Education's Resource Handbook (2015) can serve as a basis for the annual assessment:

- Does the advisory committee have a clear and concise mission statement?
- Are annual priorities established?
- Is the role of the committee clearly defined?

- Have rules or bylaws been established to identify the process for selection, term of service and the duties of committee officers?
- Have minimum standards been defined with regard to membership eligibility, term of service, attendance and a minimum number of meetings?
- Do meeting agendas reflect the role and responsibilities of the committee?
- Is the program of work/activities realistic in scope?
- Were specific timelines established for each activity?
- Are committee recommendations considered and a response provided by the school or college?
- Has the committee seen a result (improvement from implementation of recommendations)?
- Are there additional recommendations concerning the organization, membership and activities of the advisory committee?
- Are individual members' time and expertise valued by the committee and the school?
- How do advisory members rate the effectiveness of the committee?

The Nebraska Department of Education's *Developing a Local Advisory Committee Resource Handbook* is available at www.education.ne.gov/nce/Publications.html.

The majority of schools offering CTE provide standard agendas for their CTE teachers. Schools include topics that are important to the school and common to every CTE program such as enrollment and student performance data, the status of school improvement, facility modernization and new programs. The school leadership usually addresses the membership of the OACs at the beginning of the meeting to provide a brief update on school issues and successes. The agenda should include the standard welcome, approval of the previous meeting minutes, old business, new business and a motion for adjournment.

Typically, the CTE advisory committees' twice-yearly meetings focus on slightly different topics. During the fall meeting, instructors provide updates to the committee on school, program and student performance measures and placement of graduates. In addition, the status of the recommendations from the previous meeting should be addressed, such as equipment purchases and needs, the results of student performance on the end-of-year test and industry credentials earned by students.

During the spring meeting, the OAC should review the curriculum task or competency list and recommend additions, modifications and tasks to be deleted. The process can be expedited when a copy of the current task list is sent to advisory committee members a few weeks in advance with specific instructions for identifying tasks and the rationale supporting their recommendations. After the task list is revised reflecting committee recommendations, additional instructional equipment and materials may be required. The cost of new equipment will have to be included in the school operating budget and, depending on the cost of the equipment, it may not be possible to address it in the budget for the next school year. The purchase of high-cost equipment may require additional funding sources, such as grant funding or donations. The total cost of all CTE program requests may have to be prioritized. The expected timeline for procuring recommended equipment must be communicated to advisory committee members as soon as possible, but no later than the next advisory committee meeting.

We thought that including some major goals of an OAC would be helpful to the new CTE teacher as a starting point. Here is a list taken from Lehigh Career and Technical School (2010) in Pennsylvania:

- Provide guidance on the curriculum for the CTE program of study (POS).
- Recommend and/or assist CTE instructors in attaining knowledge and the application of new and emerging skills (professional development).
- Provide guidance on industry trends, job market and business and industry credentials.
- Provide guidance for articulation agreements and dual enrollment or credit for NOCTI and other industry credentials offered in CTE programs.
- Provide CTE program recommendations, including facilities, equipment and instruction.
- Provide assistance on the NOCTI "end-of-program" assessment and other third-party (skill attainment) testing.
- Provide assistance to the instructor for student mentoring, job shadowing, internship placements, cooperative education and job placement.
- Provide feedback on CTE program graduates.
- Assess the facility for safety and recommend facility modifications necessary to meet industry standards and accreditation.
- Advise on marketing and communicating educational and career opportunities to students and the community.
- Assist in securing industry-specific classroom instructional resources.
- Assist in identifying new instructors, where appropriate.
- Provide guidance in evaluating the quality of the program.

Some of these goals and their benefits are mentioned in the reflection from this Pennsylvania plumbing teacher. He calls this reflection: "CTE teachers listen up!"

Your former industry peers are your best source for help within your program. They are your program's primary "stakeholders." They will be the companies and employers that will be hiring a large percentage of the graduates from your program. Getting quality OAC members in your program is essential for the growth, stability, equipment recommendations and content accuracy within your program. Participation in your OAC lets them convey what they feel is important for student success.

That same instructor provided some hints for recruiting quality OAC members. He also spent some time talking about the benefits of participation.

Membership recruiting is never easy. Employers are very busy and getting their attention can be challenging. Make a list of business people you met when you were in the industry or knew through area trade organizations. This can be a great place to start your recruiting efforts. If your school does not have pamphlets or handouts explaining the benefits of membership for your OAC, start making one specific to your program. My discipline is Plumbing and Heating, so I looked up all of the Licensed Master Plumbers in the area and sent out a mailer to them. I followed up with a phone call. Yes this takes time, but if you want a quality program, you need to go the extra mile. Get them invited to a meeting and if you feel they can add quality to your OAC, then give them an application. I use the word 'quality' because your program needs people who are passionate about the industry in your area and are willing to help you. I have also recruited by standing at supply houses handing out pamphlets on Saturdays and on my summer days off. Find out when a supply house is doing training and be there. Most wholesalers/vendors will let you have the floor for three to five minutes to speak about your program. Join local, state and national associations in your industry too. It's a great way to discover good people.

Some benefits that you can promote to potential members can include some of these:

- Participation in NOCTI proctoring provides an opportunity to watch a student working under pressure. It is a good way for employers to find the best potential employees.
- Members are provided an opportunity to have a voice in the education and training of students for the industry. Participation

allows them to share what they feel is important for your students to know to be successful.

- Meetings create camaraderie among the members and you the teacher.
- Members can influence safety and equipment needs within your program, thereby ensuring the students are learning what is considered the industry standard.
- OAC members are generally the first contacts when it comes time for job shadowing and cooperative education placements.

Lastly, we thought we would wrap up this chapter with a reflection on the importance of an OAC from this carpentry teacher in Pennsylvania. It focuses on performance testing and how an OAC can come to your rescue.

Early in my teaching career our school administration had informed us that we would be starting a new testing program, NOCTI. NOCTI was made up of two parts, a written test and an actual performance test and was to be given to students who had finished their three years with me. We were to ask our OAC members for help. Having only experienced a few OAC meetings, I knew this discussion was going to be difficult. At the time, the various OACs met in the evening with a large group dinner and an orientation before meetings in individual labs. The administration provided the help needed to coordinate the performance test undertaking and explained all the positives for our students. I have to admit I began the meeting with a bit of apprehension, but soon we were analyzing the requirements of the performance exam and if I thought our students were ready. I was amazed at the deep discussion about carpentry skills and their support for an objective analysis of student competence. I was even more amazed when most of the committee volunteered to help with the performance testing. After the "big day," I was surprised that members of my committee had started to spread the word about the quality of students in our local carpentry program when measured on a national performance test. From then on, our OAC meetings had a clear instructional focus and even more importantly a focus on continually making my program better so that 'our' students can be successful!

KEY LEARNINGS:

1. Advisory committees are a required component of quality CTE programs.
2. Generally, there are two tiers of advisory committees.
3. OACs provide critical input for CTE teachers
4. New OAC members should be contacted personally by the CTE teacher.
5. OAC member involvement in a variety of activities is key to their engagement.
6. The major goals of an occupational advisory committee should be evaluated annually.

RELATED CONTENT THAT MAY BE OF INTEREST:

Articles

Lehigh Career and Technical School (2010). *Lehigh Career & Technical Institute Policy Manual.* Bethlehem, PA: Author. Available at www.lcti. org/uploads/LCTIPolicyManual.pdf.

Nebraska Department of Education. (2015). *Developing a Local Advisory Committee Resource Handbook.* Lincoln, NE: Author. Available at www.education.ne.gov/nce/Publications.html.

Pawlowski, B. & Meeder, H. (2012). *Building Advisory Boards That Matter.* Alexandria, VA: ACTE.

Riverside Community College. (2006). *Occupational Education Advisory Committee Handbook.* Riverside, CA: author. Available at http://asccc.org/sites/default/files/Occ_Ed_Cmte_Handout.pdf.

chapter X
End-of-Year Responsibilities

Do you know the way back to the future?

"I made it! My first year is in the books. I love teaching but I need time this summer to 'recharge' and to reflect and sort out the experiences of my first year. If I only knew then what I know now, I would have done some things differently."

Reflecting on the past year of teaching experiences helps all teachers learn from their successes and mistakes, regardless of whether they are beginning their second year of teaching or returning for their 22nd year. Each year is different and teachers learn from their collective experiences (Middleton, Abrams & Seaman, 2011). In addition, the art and science of teaching and learning continually changes. National, state and local school leaders change positions routinely and every leader champions their own educational reform initiative focusing on their priorities and new strategies. The intent of every educational reform initiative, though, is to improve instruction and student achievement. New educational initiatives and strategies provide opportunities to learn and apply additional ways for teachers to improve what they do in the classroom. It is no different in the world of business and industry, with technological change and new leadership creating new initiatives designed to increase productivity, profitability and/or customer service. Educators must continue to learn and apply new techniques just as the professionals in other career fields must.

One of the best ways for a new teacher to improve as a professional is to engage in self-reflection on the entire year of teaching. The goal of any professional is to make continuous improvement and to enhance knowledge, skills and personality traits reinforcing strengths and correcting weaknesses. A professional educator who engages in self-reflection during and after each year and strives for perfection is taking a good first step toward continued improvement.

Cochran and Reese (2013) discuss how new CTE teachers can receive valuable feedback from their mentor teachers by seeking the mentor's honest assessment and observations about their first year of teaching. It is an excellent way to gain insight from a teacher leader and to compare the mentor's feedback to the teacher's own self-reflection. Mentor teachers should provide specific observations and recommendations. It needs to be something more specific than, "You had a great year!" A mentor's comments need to focus on the new teacher's organizational skills, preparation, classroom management, instructional technique, student reaction and the new teacher's interaction with staff and others. Mentor teachers should provide specific recommendations on how to improve the areas identified. Comments need to be focused in order to help to make measurable improvements.

The formal evaluation conducted by the CTE teacher's immediate supervisor will provide a summative assessment about the teacher's performance and it should include specific commendations and recommendations for improvement. The formal evaluation and follow-up conference with a supervisor should include an opportunity for the teacher to talk about his/her self-reflection. The supervisor may have observed a CTE teacher informally during brief visits to the classroom and lab many times throughout the school year, each time observing the way the teachers engages in a variety of teaching and learning activities. In some cases, the supervisor may spend only one hour observing a lesson or lab activity during the entire school year as part of the scheduled or formal evaluation, but the year-end or summative evaluation should be a combination of both informal and formal assessments.

The amount of time spent with the mentor teacher and/or the time spent by a supervisor in a CTE lab or classroom can vary greatly depending on several factors. Time spent with a mentor (if you have access to one) can be impacted by the mentor's class load, teaching assignment, distance from the mentee and the nature of the support needed by the new teacher. Time spent with your supervisor may be impacted by the number of teachers assigned to the supervisor and by how many other new teachers may need additional support. The early indications of a new teacher's ability will determine the nature and amount of time and assistance he/she will receive from the mentor and/or the supervisor.

Considering that the total amount of time spent with a mentor and supervisor may be a small percentage of the total teaching time during the course of the year, this input is invaluable in helping a new teacher develop into a professional educator. However, self-reflection is often even more critical than the mentor's suggestions and the summative evaluation by a supervisor. Teachers should be honest in their self-assessment and make a list of areas in which they were not satisfied with their performance during the year. New teachers should have a discussion with their mentor about their self-reflection on the year and ask for specific recommendations from their mentor and/or supervisor.

Student recognition

Just prior to the end of the school year, CTE teachers must take the time necessary to meet with every student who will return and let each of them know how he or she is doing in the CTE program. The conversation should focus on students' career goals and how they can prepare to achieve them during the coming year. Returning students should know about any anticipated program changes, such as new or additional instructional equipment and additions to the curriculum. Sharing future program plans builds interest and excitement among students.

Some CTE teachers prepare a summer newsletter or electronic update about their program in which they highlight student successes and expected program changes for the start of the new school year. A newsletter, like those talked about in Chapter VII, is an effective and inexpensive way to maintain contact with students, parents and advisory committee members. Advisory committee members should also be recognized for their service in the newsletter.

Recognizing each senior at senior awards or graduation ceremonies is important, but graduation ceremony agendas and time available may restrict CTE teachers' ability to provide public recognition to every graduating senior. In some schools, CTE teachers may be permitted to provide special recognition to only one or two high-achieving students. Nevertheless, all program graduates should leave the CTE program with a skill certificate signed by their CTE teacher and/or the school leader. When possible, students should also be recognized for their performance on technical assessments, such as those offered by NOCTI, and other industry-recognized credentials. Scholarships, special awards and medals earned at CTSO competitions may also be a source of recognition. Recognition of student accomplishment is important to students, their families, employers, OAC members and to the reputation of the CTE program and school.

Management activities

Discussion about improving instruction through reflection and about the importance of recognizing and rewarding student effort does not change the fact that the nitty-gritty work of taking care of the lab and classroom facility is always going to be part of the teacher's responsibility. Most schools have a year-end checklist that identifies specific items requiring the teacher's attention prior to departure at the end of the school year. The school list usually has a timeline for the various end-of-year requirements that need to be fulfilled. In large schools, a signature may even be required by several supervisors or department leaders showing that required items have been completed. Teachers should not wait until the last minute to complete these end-of-year requirements. Although many items can be completed prior to the last day of class, the process should not interfere with planned instruction. It is important to be thorough and timely when completing year-end requirements.

Generally, end-of-year school close-out procedures include a lengthy list of items that need to be addressed in order to facilitate an orderly and timely closing of the current school year as well as to provide essential planning for the next school year. Some items act as reminders for teachers or as a self-check for items that require the teacher's response. Other items include specific requirements from various administrative offices and department heads, some of which may require teachers' initials, others may require physical items to be completed or turned in to the requestor. For instance, the administrative office may require several inventories from instructional supplies and textbooks to tool and equipment inventories. The administrative office may also request keys be turned in for classrooms, labs and storage cabinets. In addition, teachers may be asked to provide facility and equipment maintenance requests, purchase requests for supplies and equipment and copy requests for the start of the new school year. Other items may also be required, such as budget worksheets, copies of any bills owed by students and student (access) identification cards.

The curriculum department or supervisor may request a copy of curriculum revisions prepared by teachers in support of the POS. Some schools provide a specific format for the development of curriculum materials, such as learning activity packets or guides that identify all supporting instructional materials. It is common for CTE teachers to be assigned specific components of the CTE curriculum they must develop or modify during the year.

The information technology (IT) department may request maintenance requests for computers, printers and audio visual equipment; the technology department may require the location for new equipment to be installed, and take requests for courseware to be installed on administrative and instructional computers. The IT department will require that all equipment be configured for summer storage and service and all usernames and passwords need to be provided.

Other departments, such as student services, may require specific information about students. The human resources department may request information about projected changes to personal or family status for payroll and insurance purposes. Finally, the facilities maintenance department may request your instructions for equipment installation, painting and other special needs.

End-of-year checkout procedures may seem cumbersome, but they are essential for the completion of the current school-year operations and instruction. They are also important for the institution's final preparations for a cohesive start of the new school year.

Last, but not least important, CTE teachers should organize student and instructional files and clean up their own instructional area before leaving for the summer. Leaving a clean instructional area and sending a brief "thank you" note to the custodial and support staff will go a long way in gaining a little extra support in the future.

Party time (not so fast)

You aren't the only one who had a great year! Your students really helped; they advanced as you got better, so why not celebrate! It seems like the right thing to do. But if you are considering an end-of-the-year celebration with students, it would be prudent to check with the school administration to find out if a year-end party is permitted and what the school guidelines for celebrations are. Teachers should not entertain an idea or agree to do something for students that cannot be delivered. Violating school rules at the end of the year is the quickest way to end a great year of teaching with a big problem.

CTE teachers do not want their students to tell their parents, friends and other teachers that they are not doing anything in their technical program but cleaning the lab and/or having parties. The last day of school for CTE students should be a bit more relaxed, but still be a day of meaningful activity. Both new and veteran CTE teachers can find this challenging to their instructional creativity.

Preparation over the summer (recharge)

Immediately after the school year ends is the best time to send congratulatory notes or email messages to graduating seniors. Congratulate them on their accomplishments and ask a few recent graduates to serve on the occupational advisory committee or to attend an advisory meeting scheduled for the next school year. Recent CTE program graduates are an excellent resource for information about individual learning experiences in their CTE program and they can reflect on how well they were prepared for their first job and/or college. They can provide invaluable feedback about their training—including strengths and weaknesses—to perform specific tasks required on the job. Their assessment of their preparedness is usually one of the most valid assessments of the CTE program curriculum and instruction. Over the summer, a visit to the workplace of recent

graduates is another method of gathering information that can be used in preparing for the following year.

After the "thank you" notes and congratulatory messages have been sent, CTE teachers need to take time to recharge the mind and body. The first few years of teaching CTE can be very stressful and exhausting. For many CTE teachers the transition from business and industry to the classroom may have been only a few days. In some instances it is an overnight transition resulting in "mechanic today and teacher tomorrow." The transition is not a simple job change— it is a career change; the knowledge and skill sets involved in teaching a CTE subject are very different from the knowledge and skills required in industry. The business and industry knowledge and skills brought to the CTE classroom and lab are the essential "trade" background and expertise necessary to teach the specific occupational subject. However, teaching an occupational subject requires far different knowledge and skills sets.

Teaching a CTE program requires a combination of classroom management and instructional strategies on the one hand and lab or shop organizational skills and related instructional strategies on the other hand. Many effective instructional strategies apply to both the classroom and lab setting, but some strategies may be more effective in the classroom than in the lab and vice versa. The lab setting is where the concepts taught in the classroom are applied during processes, in the making of products or equipment components and/or in dealing with customers. Both classroom theory and lab application are critical to each other, enabling students to understand, apply and master the content and effectively perform a task.

It is not uncommon for new or nearly new CTE teachers to feel some disappointment or frustration over their inability to achieve all of their goals in the various aspects of teaching. Some disappointment or frustration is normal and it can be eliminated early in the new school year by taking time to prepare for the coming one. Preparation involves planning and using lessons learned during the previous year. As mentioned earlier, it requires personal reflection or self-evaluation, input from supervisors and mentors, and it is helpful to review student performance data.

Sending welcome letters to new and returning students just prior to the start of the new school year is an excellent way to establish a positive relationship and set high expectations. Similarly, most school administrators and leaders send welcome letters to new and returning staff members informing them of in-service activities prior to the first day of classes. Letters sent to staff and/or students also provide an excellent opportunity to bring attention to school and/or program priorities and to the importance of the start of the new school year. Getting a great start to the new school year sets the expectations for the rest of the year.

Planning for the future—the classroom

In addition to the activities inherent in "big picture" planning, preparing for the new school year also has to do with physical preparation of one's classroom space. CTE teachers must plan and prepare for instruction in the same manner, regardless of whether they are a new teacher or a veteran teacher with many years of experience. While CTE teachers all use the same basic planning and preparatory tools, the method in which they utilize those tools can vary greatly depending on experience, skill level and personality traits. Teachers returning for their second or third year of teaching can use their time during the summer months to adjust their plans for instruction based on the lessons learned during their previous year of instructing.

Day-to-day lesson plans and student learning activities have to be sequenced in a manner that is logical with regard to the complexity of the knowledge and skills of the occupation. Those with only one or two years of teaching experience may require additional insight or suggestions from a mentor to plan for multiple levels of instruction each day (Burns & Schaefer, 2002). Textbooks and school-provided programs of study are helpful tools that are designed to provide the minimum requirements for curriculum. They do not address the differences in instructional resources, student demographics and additional tasks that may be recommended by the occupational advisory committee. In addition, CTE teachers bring diverse personalities and unique experiences to the classroom that impact what and how the program is taught.

The first few years of teaching in CTE can be a challenge for all of the reasons mentioned previously, but most CTE teachers do exceptionally well providing a logical sequence of instruction; you will too! New CTE teachers usually approach their program by teaching units of instruction that are sequenced from least difficult to most complex, and they provide practical applications for every unit of instruction. In other words, CTE educators teach students theoretic concepts, systems or major areas of the occupation and also teach students how to perform the tasks or competencies associated with each unit, system or major area.

The end of the year is the best time to revisit plans for teaching the entire course. Planning for the next year is much easier after the first year is completed. At year's end, CTE teachers have a good idea of how much material can be covered and what instructional strategies work best with their students. Preparing for the next year can now be based on a year of experience and the plan will be more realistic. Many CTE teachers use a plan book or planning guide to help them plan instruction for the year and to gauge their progress against projected milestones for their students' progress.

Teachers can begin planning instruction for the upcoming year by mapping or scheduling the major instructional units of the course on next year's school calendar. Major units of instruction can vary in length and complexity; therefore, the amount of instructional time allocated must be proportionate to the estimated amount of time necessary for the CTE teacher to teach the unit and for students to perform and master tasks/competencies. As an example, the amount of time required for teaching a specific unit of instruction may be nine hours of theory and 21 hours of technical skill development, for a total of 30 hours for instruction and student performance on the supporting tasks or competencies. The plan book for this unit of instruction should reflect the schedule for the theory behind the competency or performance, the approximate time allocated for each class and the estimated amount of time and days/dates to complete specific tasks or competencies. Each year of teaching experience will help the teacher to make more accurate time estimates in the plan book, except that no two groups of students learn in the same way and in the same timeframe. Every class and every year is different and the estimates or milestones should be used as a guide only.

Student mastery is more important than the allocated time for various units of instruction, yet students must gain a sense of urgency to learn CTE content and skills. Creating a sense of urgency for learning encourages students to go beyond minimal competency. Enriching the learning experience beyond that minimum can help motivate learners.

Planning for the year of instruction and using a tool such as a plan book or planning guide helps teachers to stay on schedule for completing the yearly program of instruction. However, the task of planning becomes more complex when the CTE teacher has more than one grade level or multiple levels in class at one time.

The amount of time students have scheduled in CTE can vary between states and schools, with CTE classes ranging from 90 minutes to three hours each day, the average being two hours each day. If students attend class for two hours each day for 180 days each year, the amount of time available is 360 hours each year. If the CTE course is three years, 1,080 hours are available for instruction. Some CTE teachers are responsible for one year of instruction and others may be responsible for two, three or four years of instruction. Knowing the amount of time available for instruction is the first element required for planning. The second element is the number of years in the CTE program. The final element needed to plan instruction is the most important—the program of study for the CTE program.

The value of the plan book or guide is in the process. Taking time to visualize and schedule instruction and student learning activities for an entire year prepares the CTE teacher for every day of class. The planning process is ongoing and essential to teacher preparation, and preparation is the key to success in teaching and student achievement.

Planning for the future—beyond the classroom

Education is a profession and like any other profession, there are various rungs on the career ladder. Each level or job title represents a potential career goal or level of accomplishment. Teaching and administration are the two most common occupations within the profession of education.

Most career technical educators begin their careers in education as a teacher (Asunda, 2011), and the majority of CTE teachers enjoy educating students and retire only after many years. Being a great CTE teacher is an ideal career goal for many in education. Others decide to prepare for school administration and finish their careers in education as a school leader.

Regardless of their individual career goal, CTE teachers need to plan their career progression just as they plan for their yearly teaching assignment. Continuous improvement as a CTE teacher requires self-reflection and regular participation in professional development activities, both school-sponsored and personal professional experiences selected by the teacher (Bock, 2013).

Planning career progression should begin early in the teaching career. For some educators it begins while in college and for others it begins at some point during employment in a technical or service occupation. In some instances, it changes after a number of years in a teaching career. The decision to continue as a CTE teacher or to pursue a position beyond the classroom as a CTE administrator is a decision that must be made based on the interests and aspirations of the individual teacher and his/her family.

Tools for your toolbox

Teachers often struggle with utilizing instructional time effectively. How do you make every day count, especially the last day? In a CTE classroom, that last instructional day needs to be a bridge to next year's instruction and should help maintain some level of learning over the time away from instruction. Here is an example from a very creative teacher.

The last day of class can be an awkward time, as students are aware that you are trying to clean up the labs, calculate grades and pack up classroom supplies. To add to the excitement, many students are closing out their sports programs, music concerts and academic awards banquets. To keep the focus on learning, I implemented a unique last day project that helped students reflect on their experience and prepare for their future. As a graphics teacher, I assigned one semester project for each student to design and print a postcard that marketed the high school in a distinct way. Some students used pictures of the buildings and classrooms, while others took pictures of their friends and school events. The project was intended to teach design, layout and printing techniques. After the assignment was complete, I saved all the postcards and gave them back to each student on the last day of class with the following assignment: "Please address the card with your current mailing address and write yourself a note describing your current career goals. Include in the note the steps you hope to accomplish over the summer to meet those goals." Then through the summer I read the cards, included a note of my own and dropped the notes in the mail. You would be amazed at how many students stopped by the following year to say they received their postcard and proceeded to tell me about what they did to work toward their goals. The entire activity is intended to help students reflect on their time in my class and think about how what they are accomplishing in school will help them throughout their lives.

 We believe that honest reflection is a great way to consistently improve one's craft and that includes the craft of teaching. Here's an example from a former Wisconsin CTE teacher that we thought you would enjoy. He calls it, "A Look in the Rearview Mirror."

It has been many years since I was a first-year teacher, but that does not mean those days are not still clear in my mind. As a new teacher there are many responsibilities and expectations that require your attention, time and professional focus. Some of these responsibilities, such as curriculum development, classroom management and student academic progress are practiced and embedded in the pedagogy of teacher preparation programs. Whether you are a first-year teacher coming through a university certification program or if you took a non-traditional path of alternative certification, the following reflections may serve as guideposts for continued success.

First and foremost, take pride in knowing that you have entered an honorable and important position in influencing the lives of youth. A teacher provides a compass for personal and academic growth for youth and adults. Your knowledge, skills and life experiences serve as stabilizers for the content you teach and the manner in which you deliver that content. After my first year, I was relieved just to have made it to graduation, but now that I reflect on what technique helped me prepare for my career, I know it was the challenges that I faced each year that made me a better teacher the following year. After each year and often at the mid-year break, I used a journal to document what worked and what could have been improved. Simple notes on classroom demonstrations, levels of supplies needed, test questions and student engagement were used in preparing lesson plans for the next group of students. This type of continuous improvement model will allow you to reduce mistakes, build confidence about what you are trying to convey to students and prepare your lab/lesson for student success. This simple effort to record reflections allowed me to look at the lessons from a fresh perspective without losing the ideas that may have been generated at a time of high stress or impact.

The classroom improvement strategy of keeping a journal played a big part in reducing my planning time and stress about how successful lab activities were for students. To reinforce my practice and classroom management perspective, I also developed a peer mentoring relationship with fellow teachers who had several years of experience and had earned the respect of students, administration and the community. I shared my journal notes with my mentors and added their perspective. Since I had little experience, I was not always sure when student results should be classified as average or poor. It was easy to tell when the lesson went great, but I wanted to better understand the intersection between individual student success and collective group or class success. My mentors had many more years of experience that helped to balance my desire to think I frequently had to adjust teaching to improve chances of student success. Oftentimes, our conversations focused on teaching techniques, student preparedness and alternative ways to assess student progress. These conversations were also a great way to learn about the culture of the school and community. My advice for a new teacher is this: becoming a successful teacher is proportional to the level of commitment you make to becoming a student of your profession.

We also wanted to supply you with a generic end-of-year checklist; though these vary greatly by type of program and school, it may provide a good starting point.

- Put your name on any classroom item that you wish to keep for next year. For example, if you are leaving your files at school in a file cabinet, make sure to put masking tape with your name on it on the file cabinet. Items have a tendency to "leave" if they are not marked.
- Clean up your classroom. While the desks and floors will be swept and washed by the janitorial staff over the summer, it is your responsibility to make sure bulletin boards, countertops and desks are cleared and that supplies are stored and clearly labeled.
- Complete and submit a classroom repair list.
- Return all audio-visual equipment.
- Clean up computer files, deleting and organizing as necessary.
- Return teacher laptops or check them out for the summer.
- Return to the media center any resources you have checked out.
- Turn in senior failure lists.
- Turn in final grades.
- Turn in your official grade book.
- Return keys (as per policy).

KEY LEARNINGS:

1. Reflection on past accomplishments at year's end is a great step toward continuous improvement.
2. Compare your end-of-year reflections with those of a supervisor, mentor or peer.
3. Student recognition is a "must-do" at the end of the year.
4. Follow all year-end closeout procedures.
5. Think about the implications of end-of-year "parties."
6. Don't forget to say "thanks!"
7. Plan for instruction.
8. Plan for your own career advancement.

RELATED CONTENT THAT MAY BE OF INTEREST:

Articles

Asunda, P. (2011). Career and Technical Education Teacher Preparation Trends. *Online Journal for Workforce Education and Development,* (V)3. Available at http://opensiuc.lib.siu.edu/cgi/viewcontent.cgi?article=1107&context=ojwed.

Bock, S. (2010, January). Teacher recognition. *Techniques.* (85)1.

Burns, J. Z. & Schaefer, K. (2002). From Technician to Reflective Practitioner. (40)1. Available at http://scholar.lib.vt.edu/ejournals/JITE/v40n1/burns.html.

Cochran, L. & Reese, S. (2007). A Successful Induction into the Teaching Profession. *Techniques.* (82)9.

Middleton, M., Abrams, E. & Seaman. J. (2011). Resistance and Dis-identification in Reflective Practice with Preservice Teaching Interns. *New Directions for Teaching and Learning,* No. 126, 67-75.

Conclusion

In our "Setting the Stage" introduction we talked about the "specialness" of new CTE teachers and reiterated that those entering through an alternative certification are truly a "special breed." The numerous differences between these educators and other traditionally prepared educators include differences in prior work experience, work environments and operating a safe environment in which students can learn. Although there are many books on teaching strategies, quite a few on tips for new teachers, we are aware of none focused on new CTE teachers who have come primarily from alternative certification programs.

We hope this book—especially when coupled with our first book—has shed some light on some of the details of becoming a CTE professional. *Your First Year in CTE: 10 Things to Know* focused most heavily on the importance of relationship building, not only with your students, but also with your peers and supervisors. The content of this book concentrates on more detailed issues such as the importance of planning, assessing students or your work and using external relationships to enhance your ability to prepare students for a successful future.

Throughout the book we tried our best to maintain a short, simple, focused but lighthearted, resource that pays attention to helping the new CTE teacher. We utilized chapter titles that show our focus first and then we included a subtitle that we hoped you'd find funny but analogous to your current situation. We really appreciated our reader's comments from the previous book regarding inclusion of teacher reflections and usable examples from real classrooms; we have included many of them in a section called "Tools for your toolbox." The "tools" section is near the end of every chapter (just before "Key Learnings" and "Resources") and we have included a minimum of three "tools" with each chapter.

We would also encourage each of you to think about submitting something to us directly or to be posted on ACTE's website that would be of benefit to your peers, kind of a "pay-it-forward" approach. Lastly, as we have done with previous chapters and with our last book, we want to provide you with a list of key points for the overall book, so in no particular order, here we go!

- Get your bearings regarding the overall direction of your technical content. Are you using guidelines for state standards, programs of study, industry association standards (carefully verify these), a textbook, your own experience or some combination of any of these?

- Understand the benefits of annual planning and consider incorporating projects that encompass a number of different competencies. Include not only technical competencies but also academic and workplace foundational ones, and consider something that will benefit the greater community.

- Day-to-day planning is critical to your survival.

- Career and technical student organizations provide benefits for students and the teacher leaders. They provide a co-curricular mechanism for extending student learning beyond the school day, to reinforce learning, teach leadership skills, motivate students and encourage student success.

- Student assessment serves as a benchmark and a measure of determining student competence. Assessment can take many forms and measure many things, but it is important for both you and your students to see it as positive and equitable.

- Data from student assessments are one of the best ways to continuously improve your program. These data can improve your instruction, the projects and resources you select, as well as your overall ability as a CTE teacher.

- Parents can be your biggest allies. Find ways to maintain positive communications with them about your program and about their son or daughter.

- Become skilled in ways to enhance learning for all students, including those with special needs. Familiarize yourself with applicable requirements of the IEP process. Instructional changes made for students with special needs can improve the instruction you provide for all of your students.

- Occupational Advisory Committees can be your strongest advocate. Communicate often with these practicing content experts and be sure to find time to both thank and reward them for their expertise.

- Take time to reflect as you conclude your first year. It is an important time to self-assess on the progress you've made as a CTE teacher and how you can improve even further.

The authors and the contributing authors really hope you find this book useful and that you will consider placing your "Toolbox tools" on ACTE's website found at www.acteonline.org/FirstYearInCTE. We plan to explore an additional 10 topics that CTE teachers can use soon and it would be great to use your examples!

Contributing Authors

The authors would like to both recognize and thank the following individuals for their contributions to this book. These individuals provided the contacts, reflections and templates for our "Tools for your toolbox" "section. Sometimes the authors of this book even supplied their own reflections. These individuals are not only experts, but they are also dedicated to CTE and its continuous improvement. We are proud to call them both colleagues and friends.

Bryan D. Albrecht, Ed. D.
Gateway Technical College, WI

Gregory G. Belcher, Ph.D.
Pittsburg State University, Technical Teacher Education, KS

Jonathan Bibb, B.S.
Administrator, Arkansas career Training Institute, AR

Suzanne M. Nocchi-Dill, M.Ed
Capital School District,Culinary Arts Instructor, DE

H. Jason Fogleman
Cumberland Perry AVTS, Precision Machining Teacher, PA

Danielle N. Grant
Buffalo High School, FFA Advisor, WV

Dennis D. Harden, Ed. D.
Elementary and Secondary Education Coordinator, Career Education, MO

Edward R. Hensley, M.S.
Olathe Advanced Technical Center, Automotive Instructor, KS

Paula M. Hudis, Ph.D.
ConnectEd, Director of Institutional Development, CA

Dexter Johnigan, MAFM, MCTS
Tucker Middle School, FBLA Adviser, GA

Cynthia Brennan-Jones, Ph.D.
Indian River State College, Learning Facilitator, FL

Dave A. McCall, M. Ed
Ferris State University, Professor, MI

Ellen Nutter, M. Ed.
Chester County IU, Pickering, Early Childhood Care & Education Instructor, PA

Diana T. Penn, CEPC, CCE
Upper Bucks CTC, Pastry Chef Instructor, Pennsylvania

Steven D. Polley, M.S.
Pittburg State University, Automotive Technology, KS

Jill R. Shurtleff
Warwick Career and Technical Center, Cosmetology Instructor, RI

Dawn Simpson, Ed.D.
Director of Vocational Training, Arkansas career Training Institute, AR

Ann M. Thomas, CCI
Academy of Careers and Technology, Cosmetology Instructor, WV

Brenda L. Tuckwiller, Ed.D.
WVU Institute of Technology, Teacher Education, WV

Delmas L. Watkins, Ed.D.
CTAE Director, DeKalb County School District, GA

Russell P. Weikle, M.A.
State CTE Director, CA

Contributing Organizations

The authors would like to both recognize and thank ACTE and NOCTI for their contributions and assistance with this book. Unlike the individuals recognized in the previous section, these entities provided the authors with the opportunity to expand upon their individual knowledge and skills, and have indirectly influenced much of the content of this book through conversations and interviews with their members and clients. In addition, these organizations have contributed resources, both human and financial, to make this book a reality.

ACTE (The Association for Career and Technical Education)

The Association for Career and Technical Education is the largest national education association in the United States dedicated to the advancement of education that prepares youth and adults for careers. ACTE was founded in 1926 and it has remained committed to enhancing the job performance and satisfaction of its members; to increasing public awareness and appreciation for career and technical education (CTE); and to assuring growth in local, state and federal funding for these programs by communicating and working with legislators and government leaders.

NOCTI (Formerly the National Occupational Competency Testing Institute)

NOCTI is an assessment organization that was founded in the mid-1960s as a not-for-profit entity serving the CTE field through a consortium made up of career technical education directors (or their designees) from each state and U.S. territories. NOCTI shares the objective of other CTE associations, including the Association for Career and Education, whose membership this book is targeted to assist and the National Association of State Directors of Career and Technical Education consortium (NASDCTEc), which elect the NOCTI board of directors. All three organizations have expertise in, and a strong commitment to, improving America's workforce.

Special Thanks

Amie L. Bloomfield, B.S., NOCTI, Division Manager
for additional editing and creative development

Carol L. Hodes, Ph.D., NOCTI, Senior Consultant
for searching the literature for resources that are useful to CTE teachers

Jaclyn D. Kamp, NOCTI, Lead Graphic Designer
for her creative illustrations and suggestions

Sandra G. Pritz, Ph.D., NOCTI Senior Consultant
for many hours spent checking consistency, tone, style and grammar

Complete Resource List

ACTE. (2015) Lesson Plan Search. *Educator Resources.* Available at www.acteonline.org/lessonPlanSearch.aspx?id=131.

ACTE Factsheets. Available at www.acteonline.org/factsheets/#.Vc32ipfvfh4.

Admin. (2012, November 19). Parent Communication Log Template. *Log Templates.* Available at www.logtemplate.com/parent-communication-log.html.

Aguilar, E. (2014, November 3). *20 Tips for Developing Positive Relationships with Parents.* Jossey Bass Education. Available at http://josseybasseducation.com/teaching-learning/20-tips/.

Alfeld, C., Stone, J. R., Aragon, S. R., Hansen, D. M., Zirkle, C., Connors, J., Spindler, M, Romine, R. & Woo, H. (2007). *Looking Inside the Black Box: The Value Added by Career and Technical Student Organizations to Students' High School Experience.* St. Paul, MN: National Research Center for Career and Technical Education, University of Minnesota. Available at www.nrccte.org/sites/default/files/publication-files/looking_inside_the_black_box.pdf.

Anderson, L.W. (Ed.), Krathwohl, D.R. (Ed.), Airasian, P.W., Cruikshank, K.A., Mayer, R.E., Pintrich, P.R., Raths, J., & Wittrock, M.C. (2001). *A Taxonomy for Learning, Teaching and Assessing: A Revision of Bloom's Taxonomy of Educational Objectives* (Complete edition). New York: Longman.

Association for Career and Technical Education ACTE (2006, January). *Reinventing the American High School for the 21st Century: Strengthening a New Vision for the American High School Through the Experiences and Resources of Career and Technical Education.* A Position Paper. Alexandria, VA: Author. Available at www.acteonline.org/uploadedFiles/Assets_and_Documents/Global/files/Reinventing_American_High_School.pdf.

Association for Career and Technical Education (ACTE). (2015). History of CTE. Available at www.acteonline.org/general.aspx?id=810#.Vdx4z5fvfh4.

Association for Career Technical Education. (2011, June). Expanding Career Readiness Through Career Technical Student Organizations. Alexandria, VA: Author. Available at www.acteonline.org/WorkArea/DownloadAsset.aspx?id=2116.

Association for Career Technical Education. CTE Clearinghouse: *Career and Technical Student Organizations.* Available at www.acteonline.org/general.aspx?id=2215#.Vc35bJfvfh4.

Barlis, L. (2013, September). Relationships that Make a Difference. *Educational Leadership, 71*(1). Available at www.ascd.org/publications/educational-leadership/sept13/vol71/num01/ Relationships-That-Make-a-Difference.aspx.

Bottoms, G., Pucel, D. & Phillips, I. (1997). *Designing Challenging Vocational Courses*. Atlanta, GA: Southern Regional Education Board.

Boudett, K. P., Murnane, R. J., City, E., & Moody, L. (2005). Teaching Educators: How to Use Student Assessment Data to Improve Instruction. *Phi Delta Kappan, (86)*9, 700-706. (**ERIC Number:** EJ712938).

Brown, B. L. (1997). Task Analysis Strategies and Practices. Practice Application Brief. **ERIC Number:** ED404571. Available at http://eric.ed.gov/?id=ED404571.

BSCS. (2015). BSCS 5E Instructional Model. Videos and tools available at www.bscs.org/ bscs-5e-instructional-model.

Castellano, M., Sundell, K., Overman, L. T., & Aliaga, O. A. (2012). Do Career and Technical Education Programs of Study Improve Student Achievement? Preliminary Analyses from a Rigorous Longitudinal Study. *International Journal of Educational Reform, (21)*, 98-118. Available at www.nrccte.org/resources/external-reports/do-career-and-technical-education-programs-study-improve-student.

Center for Teaching Excellence (2015). *Teaching Styles: 7 Things to Consider About Teaching Styles*. University of South Carolina. Available at www.sc.edu/cte/guide/teachingstyles/.

Commission on Teacher Credentialing. (2009, May). *Standards of Quality and Effectiveness for Career/Technical Education Teachers*. Sacramento, CA: Author. Available at www.ctc.ca.gov/ educator-prep/standards/CTE-Handbook.pdf.

Cromey, A. (2000, November). *Using Student Assessment Data: What Can We Learn from Schools?* (Policy Issues Brief No. 6). Oakbrook, IL: National Central Regional Educational Laboratory. (**ERIC Number:** ED452593).

CTE Online. (2011). CTE Online Lesson Plan Template—Word Version. Available at http://cteteach.cteonline.org/portal/default/Resources/Viewer/ResourceViewer?action=2& resid=389264.

Curwin, R. (2015, August 12). Questions Before Answers: What Drives a Great Lesson? *Edutopia Student Engagement* blog. Available at www.edutopia.org/blog/questions-answers-drive-great-lesson-richard-curwin?utm_source=SilverpopMailing&utm_medium=email&utm_campaign=081915%20enews%20ibl%20ngm%20A&utm_content=&utm_term=top1&spMailingI D=12166634&spUserID=MjcyNjg1NDgzMDAS1&spJobID=601305544&spReportId=NjAxM zA1NTQ0S0.

Dale, E. (1969). *Audiovisual Methods in Teaching*. NY: Dryden Press. Retrieved June 11, 2015 from www.etsu.edu/uged/etsu1000/documents/Dales_Cone_of_Experience.pdf.

Dolan, L., Ford, C., Newton, V., & Kellam, S.G. (1989). *The Mastery Learning Manual*. Johns Hopkins Center for Prevention and Early Intervention. Available at www.jhsph.edu/ research/centers-and-institutes/johns-hopkins-center-for-prevention-and-early-intervention/ Publications/mlm.pdf.

Editorial Projects in Education Research Center. (2011, September 1). Issues A-Z: Technology in Education. *Education Week.* Available at www.edweek.org/ew/issues/technology-in-education./

Educational Testing Service. (2015). *How Tests and Test Questions are Developed.* Princeton, NJ: Author. Retrieved From: www.ets.org/understanding_testing/test_development/.

Ferlazzo, L. (2014, November 29). Formative Assessments are Powerful: Classroom Q&A with Larry Ferlazzo. *Education Week.* Retrieved from http://blogs.edweek.org/teachers/classroom_qa_with_larry_ferlazzo/.

Ferrara, S., Huff, K. & Lopez, E. (2010). Targeting Cognition in Item Design to Enhance Valid Interpretations of Test Performances: A Case Study and Some Speculations. A Paper Presented in S. Ferrara & K. Huff (Chairs), *Cognition and Valid Inferences about Student Achievement: Aligning Items with Cognitive and Proficiency Targets.* Denver, CO: Cognition and Assessment Special Interest Group symposium conducted at the annual meeting of the American Educational Research Association.

Fiscus, L. & Hyslop, A. (2008). *Career and Technical Student Organizations Reference Guide,* third edition. Available at www.tsaweb.org/sites/default/files/CTSO-Guide.pdf.

Fletcher Jr., E., Djajalaksana, Y., & Eison, J. (2012). Instructional Strategy Use of Faculty in Career and Technical Education. *Journal of Career and Technical Education, (27) 2, 69-75.* Available at http://files.eric.ed.gov/fulltext/EJ995896.pdf.

Foster, J., Hodes, C.L., & Pritz, S.G. (2014). Chapter VII: Analyzing the Data in *Putting Your Data to Work: Improving Instruction in CTE.* Alexandria, VA: ACTE.

Fox, L. (2015, April 1). Celebration: The Internal Motivator for Student Achievement. *The Leader in Me Blog.* Available at www.theleaderinme.org/blog/celebration-the-internal-motivator-for-student-achievement/.

Glazer, N. (2014). Formative Plus Summative Assessment in Large Undergraduate Courses: Why Both? *International Journal of Teaching and Learning in Higher Education, (26)2,* 276-286. **(ERIC Number:** EJ1060846).

Goldrick, L., Osta, D., Barlin, D. & Burn, J. (2012). *Review of State Policies of Teacher Induction.* Santa Cruz, CA: New Teacher Center. Available at www.newteachercenter.org/sites/default/files/ntc/main/resources/brf-ntc-policy-state-teacher-induction.pdf.

Greenstein, L. (2010.) *What Teachers Really Need to Know About Formative Assessment.* Alexandria, VA: ASCD. Retrieved June 11, 2015, from www.ascd.org/publications/books/110017/chapters/The-Fundamentals-of-Formative-Assessment.aspx.

Guskey, T.R. & Anderman, E. (2014). In Search of a Useful Definition of Mastery. *Educational Leadership,71*(4), 18-23. Available at www.be.wednet.edu/cms/lib2/WA01001601/Centricity/Domain/18/In%20Search%20of%20a%20Useful%20Definition%20of%20Mastery.pdf.

Halloran, J. (2015). 7 Effective Parent Teacher Communication Tips. *K 12 Teacher Alliance.* Available at www.teachhub.com/parent-teacher-communication-tips.

Hattie, J. (2003). Formative and Summative Interpretations of Assessment Information. *Who Says Formative Assessment Matters?* Retrieved from www.scribd.com/doc/50784590/2003-Hattie-Formative-and-summative-interpretations-of-assessment-information#scribd.

Herrmann, E. (2014, February 12). The Importance of Guided Practice in the Classroom. *Multi Briefs: Exclusive.* Available at http://exclusive.multibriefs.com/content/the-importance-of-guided-practice-in-the-classroom/education.

Higley, M. (2013, October 13). Benefits of Synchronous and Asynchronous. *e-Learning Industry.* Available at http://elearningindustry.com/benefits-of-synchronous-and-asynchronous-e-learning.

Hmelo-Silver, C. (2004). Problem-Based learning: What and How Do Students Learn? *Education Psychology Review,(16)* 3, 235-266. Available at http://link.springer.com/article/10.1023%2FB%3AEDPR.0000034022.16470.f3.

Hochlander, E. G, Kaufman, Levesque, P. K. & Houser, J. (1992). *Vocational Education in the United States: 1969-1990.* NCES 92-669. Washington, DC: U.S. Department of Education, Office of Educational Research and Improvement. Available at http://nces.ed.gov/pubs92/92669.pdf.

Hudis, P. & Harris, K. (2010, March 1). Getting it Right: Performance-based Curriculum Integration in Small Learning Communities Presented at the Educating for Careers Conference, California Center for College and Career, Sacramento, CA. Available at http://2010.ccpc-conference.net/sites/default/files/presentationfiles/Getting%20it%20Right%20-%20Performance-based%20Curriculum%20%28handouts%29.pdf.

Individuals with Disabilities Education Act (IDEA). Available at idea.ed.gov/explore/home and www.disability.gov/individuals-disabilitieseducation-act-idea/.

Institute of Education Science. (2015). Designing Quasi-experiments: Meeting What Works Clearinghouse Standards Without Random Assignment (Webinar transcript). Washington DC: U.S. Department of Education. Retrieved from http://ies.ed.gov/ncee/wwc/multimedia.aspx?sid=23.

Kelly, M. (2015). Whole Group Discussion Pros and Cons. *About Education.* Available at http://712educators.about.com/od/lessonplans/p/discussions.htm.

Kennedy, B. (1997). *Robert's Rules of Order*—Summary Version. Available at www.robertsrules.org/.

Krathwohl, D. R. (2002). A Revision of Bloom`s Taxonomy: An Overview. *Theory Into Practice, 41*(4), Autumn 2002. 212-218. Retrieved June 11, 2015 from www.unco.edu/cetl/sir/stating_outcome/documents/Krathwohl.pdf.

Lovgren, M. (2011). Writing Your OWN CTE Online Lesson. *CTE Online.* Available at http://cteteach.cteonline.org/portal/default/Curriculum/Viewer/Curriculum?action=2&view=viewer&cmobjid=856232.

Macdonald, H. & Teed, R.; updated by Hoyt, G, Imazeki, J., Millis, B., &Vazquez-Cognet, J. (2015, May 28). Interactive Lectures. *Pedagogy in Action.* Available at http://serc.carleton.edu/sp/library/interactive//index.html.

Mariconda, B. (2015). Five Keys to Successful Parent-Teacher Communication. *Scholastic.* Available at www.scholastic.com/teachers/article/five-keys-successful parent-teacher-communication.

Mathews, J. (2011, December 18). New Teacher Decries Lesson Plan Gap [blog post]. Retrieved from *Class Struggle* at *The Washington Post* at www.washingtonpost.com/blogs/class-struggle/post/new-teacher-decries-lesson-plan-gap/2011/12/17/gIQAt0C50O_blog.html.

Merriam-Webster. (2015). Merriam-Webster's Collegiate Dictionary. Springfield, MA: Merriam-Webster, Incorporated.

Moyer, L. (2015). Begin With the End in Mind. ACTE blog. Available at www.acteonline.org/eia.post.aspx?id=4056&blogid=2666#.Vb_rxvnvfh4.

Murray, J. (1905). *The Sayings of Lao-Tzu.* London, England: Hazell Watson and Viney, Ltd.

National Association of State Directors of Career Technical Education Consortium. (2011). *Building Comprehensive Programs of Study Through Progressive State Career and Technical Legislation.* Silver Spring, MD: National Association of State Directors of Career Technical Education. Retrieved June 11, 2015, www.careertech.org/sites/default/files/Principle4-CTE-POS-2011.pdf.

National Association of State Directors of Career Technical Education Consortium. (2015). Available at www.careertech.org/career-clusters.

National Coordinating Council for Career and Technical Student Organizations (NCC-CTSO). (2015). Available at www.ctsos.org/.

Nebraska Department of Education. (2015). *Item Writing Guidelines.* Lincoln NE: author. Retrieved June 11, 2015, from www.education.ne.gov/Assessment/pdfs/C4L/Item_Writing_Guidelines.pdf .

Newman, L., Wagner, M., Huang, T., Shaver, D., Knokey, A.-M., Yu, J., Contreras, E., Ferguson, K., Greene, S., Nagle, K., & Cameto, R. (2011). Secondary School Programs and Performance of Students with Disabilities. A Special Topic Report of Findings From the National Longitudinal Transition Study-2 (NLTS2). (NCSER 2012-3000). U.S. Department of Education. Washington, DC: National Center for Special Education Research. Available at http://ies.ed.gov/ncser/pubs/20123000/pdf/20123000.pdf.

Newman, L., Wagner, M., Knokey, A.-M., Marder, C., Nagle, K., Shaver, D., Wei, X., with Cameto, R., Contreras, E., Ferguson, K., Greene, S., & Schwarting, M. (2011). The Post-high School Outcomes of Young Adults with Disabilities Up to 8 Years After High School. A Report From the National Longitudinal Transition Study-2 (NLTS2) (NCSER 2011-3005). Menlo Park, CA: SRI International. Available at http://ies.ed.gov/ncser/pubs/20113005/pdf/20113005.pdf.

NOCTI (2015). Assessments, Blueprints. Big Rapids, MI: Author. Retrieved from www.nocti.org/Pre-Testing.cfm?m=2.

Ohio Department of Education. (2015). Career tech FAQs. Available at http://education.ohio.gov/Topics/Career-Tech/CTE-FAQ#FAQ1517.

Pashler, H., Bain, P., Bottge, B., Graesser, A., Koedinger, K., McDaniel, M. & Metcalfe, J. (2007). *Organizing Instruction and Study to Improve Student Learning* (NCER 2007-2004). Washington, DC: National Center for Education Research, Institute of Education Sciences, U.S. Department of Education. Retrieved from http://ncer.ed.gov.

Peterson, D. (2015). What is the Difference Between Asynchronous and Synchronous Learning? *About Education.* Available at http://adulted.about.com/od/glossary/g/Asynchronous-Learning.htm.

Popham, W. J. (2006). *Defining and Enhancing Formative Assessment.* Paper presented at the Annual Large-Scale Assessment Conference, Council of Chief State School Officers, San Francisco, CA.

Priceless Teaching Strategies. (2008). *Quick, Effective Parent Contact by Phone or Email!! Contact Parents by Phone.* Available at www.priceless-teaching-strategies.com/parent_contact.html.

Research & Innovation Network. (2015). *Stronger Communication.* Center for Learning Science & Technology. Available at http://researchnetwork.pearson.com/learning-science/teaching-in-a-digital-age/stronger-communication.

Ritz, G. (2014, September 16). *New CTE Teacher Resources: Parent Communications.* Indiana Department of Education. Available at www.doe.in.gov/cte/new-cte-teacher-resources.

Saavedra, A.R. & Opfer, V.D. (2012, Oct 19). Nine Lessons on How to Teach 21st Century Skills and Knowledge. *The Rand Blog.* www.rand.org/blog/2012/10/nine-lessons-on-how-to-teach-21st-century-skills-and.html.

Southern Region Education Board (SREB). (2008). *Planning for Improved Student Achievement.* Atlanta, GA: Author. Available at http://publications.sreb.org/2008/08V05_SBU_Intro.pdf.

Sparks, S. (2015, January 28). Differentiated Instruction: A Primer. *Education Week.* Available at www.edweek.org/ew/articles/2015/01/28/differentiated-instruction-a-primer.html.

States` Career Clusters Initiative. (2008). Agriculture, Food and Natural Resources Career Cluster, Plant Systems Pathways Knowledge and Skill Statements. Retrieved from www.careertech.org/sites/default/files/K%26S-CareerPathway-AG-PlantSystems-2008.pdf.

Stone, J. R. III. (2014) More Than One Way: The Case for High-quality CTE. *American Educator, (38)* 3. Issue available at www.aft.org/sites/default/files/ae_fall2014.pdf.

The Carl D. Perkins Career and Technical Education Act of 2006 (Public Law 109-270)). Available at www2.ed.gov/policy/sectech/leg/perkins/index.html.

Thiede, R. (2012). Best Practices with Online Courses. *US-China Education Review* A 2, 135-141. ERIC Number: ED532176. Available at http://files.eric.ed.gov/fulltext/ED532176.pdf.

Threeton, M., Ewing, J. & Clark, R. (2010, Summer). An Informal Analysis of Career and Technical Student Organization Competitive Event Competencies via Kolb`s Experiential Learning Theory. *Online Journal of Workforce Education and Development,* (IV)3. Available at http://opensiuc.lib.siu.edu/cgi/viewcontent.cgi?article=1079&context=ojwed.

University of South Carolina. (2015). CTE at USC: Teaching Guide—Things to Consider About Teaching. *Center for Teaching Excellence.* Available at www.sc.edu/cte/guide/teaching-styles/.

U.S. Department of Labor, Employment and Training Administration. (2006). *Testing and Assessment: A Guide to Good Practices for Workforce Investment Professionals.* Washington, DC, U.S. Department of Labor. Retrieved June 11, 2015 from www.onetcenter.org/dl_files/pro-TestAsse.pdf.

U.S. Department of Labor and Social Policy Research Associates. (2011, March). *Career Pathways Initiative: Building Cross-agency Partnerships* (webinar recording). Available at, www.workforce3one.org/view/3001107557559061701.

U.S. Department of Labor and Social Policy Research Associates. (2011, September). *Career Pathways Toolkit.* Retrieved from https://learnwork.workforce3one.org/view/2001134052969836533/info.

Utah Education Network. *K-12 Core Lesson Plans.* Available at www.uen.org/k12educator/corelessonplans.shtml.

Vocational Information Center. (2009, February 21). *Career Activities and Vocational Lesson Plans.* Available at www.khake.com/.

Waller, K. V. (2008). *Writing Instructional Objectives.* Rosemont, IL: National Accrediting Agency for Clinical Laboratory Sciences. Retrieved June 11, 2015, www.naacls.org/docs/announcement/writing-objectives.pdf.

Wang, C. & Ong, G. (2003). Questioning for Active Learning. *Ideas on Teaching.* Available at www.cdtl.nus.edu.sg/ideas/iot2.htm.

Wayne Technical & Career Center. (2015). *Communicating the Value of CTE to Parents.* Available at www.waynetechcenter.org/parents.cfm?subpage=1352294.

Webb, N. L. (1997). *Criteria for Alignment of Expectations and Assessments in Mathematics and Science Education.* Council of Chief State School Officers and National Institute for Science Education Research Monograph No. 6. Madison, WI: University of Wisconsin. Available at http://facstaff.wcer.wisc.edu/normw/WEBBMonograph6criteria.pdf.

Winston, J. (2015). Parent Communication Log. *The Teaching Oasis.* Available at www.teachingoasis.com/Parent%20Communication%20Log.pdf.

Zirkle, C. J., Martin, L., & McCaslin, N. L. (2007). *Study of State Certification Licensure Requirements for Secondary Career and Technical Education Teachers.* St. Paul, MN: National Research Center for Career and Technical Education, University of Minnesota. Retrieved from www.nrccte.org.